All rights reserved, The Breakfast Group 2012

The Breakfast Group

THE BREAKFAST GROUP

This informal association of practicing studio artist, dating back to the early 1960's originally began when a group of faculty members at the University of California at Berkeley, decided to meet regularly for breakfast at a Shattuck Avenue coffee house.

They met to discuss recent developments in the visual arts, student-related concerns and individual artistic pursuits. In the open-agenda atmosphere of breakfast, conversations would inevitably drift to such diverse areas as current events, Berkeley politics, recent films and progress of the Bay Area sports teams.

Over the years there have been a number of changes, both in the composition of the group itself and in breakfast venues. Though current members may be teaching throughout the Bay Area, exhibiting beyond these borders, they stand firm on their allegiance to Cal teams.

Artistically, THE BREAKFAST GROUP represents a wide diversity of stylistic and philosophical viewpoints. They get together out of a sense of shared purpose as visual artist in a spirit of conviviality, camaraderie, and conversation.

Spanning five decades, THE BREAKFAST GROUP has provided inspiration and encouragement to countless numbers of college art students who have gone on to make significant contributions to our community. THE BREAKFAST GROUP has been a constant touchstone for members who have enriched the arts in California and far beyond.

Robert Simons

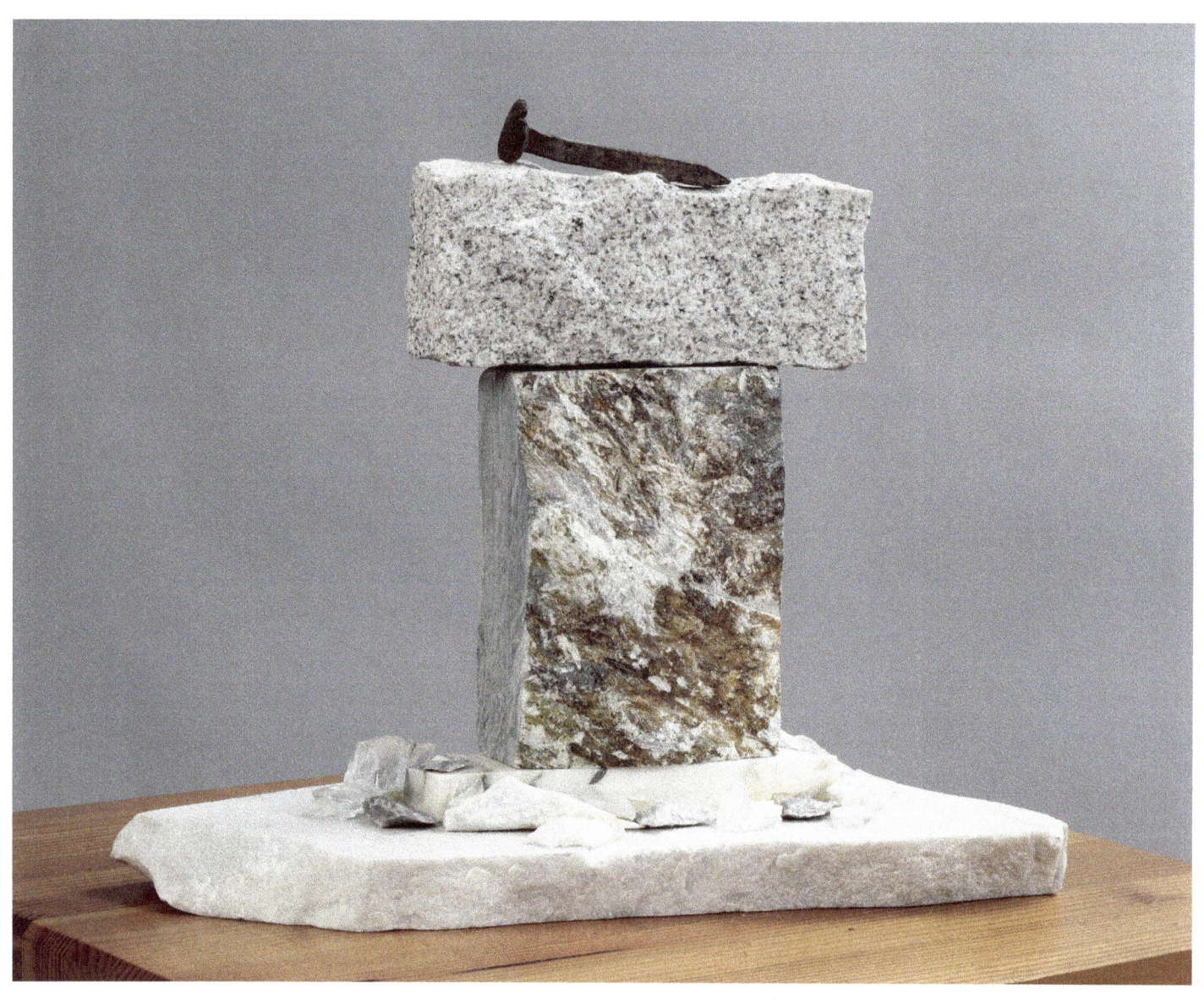

Patricia Bengston-Jones, *Long Time Ago Useful,* 2011, Steel, granite, glass and marble, 13 x 17 x 11 in.

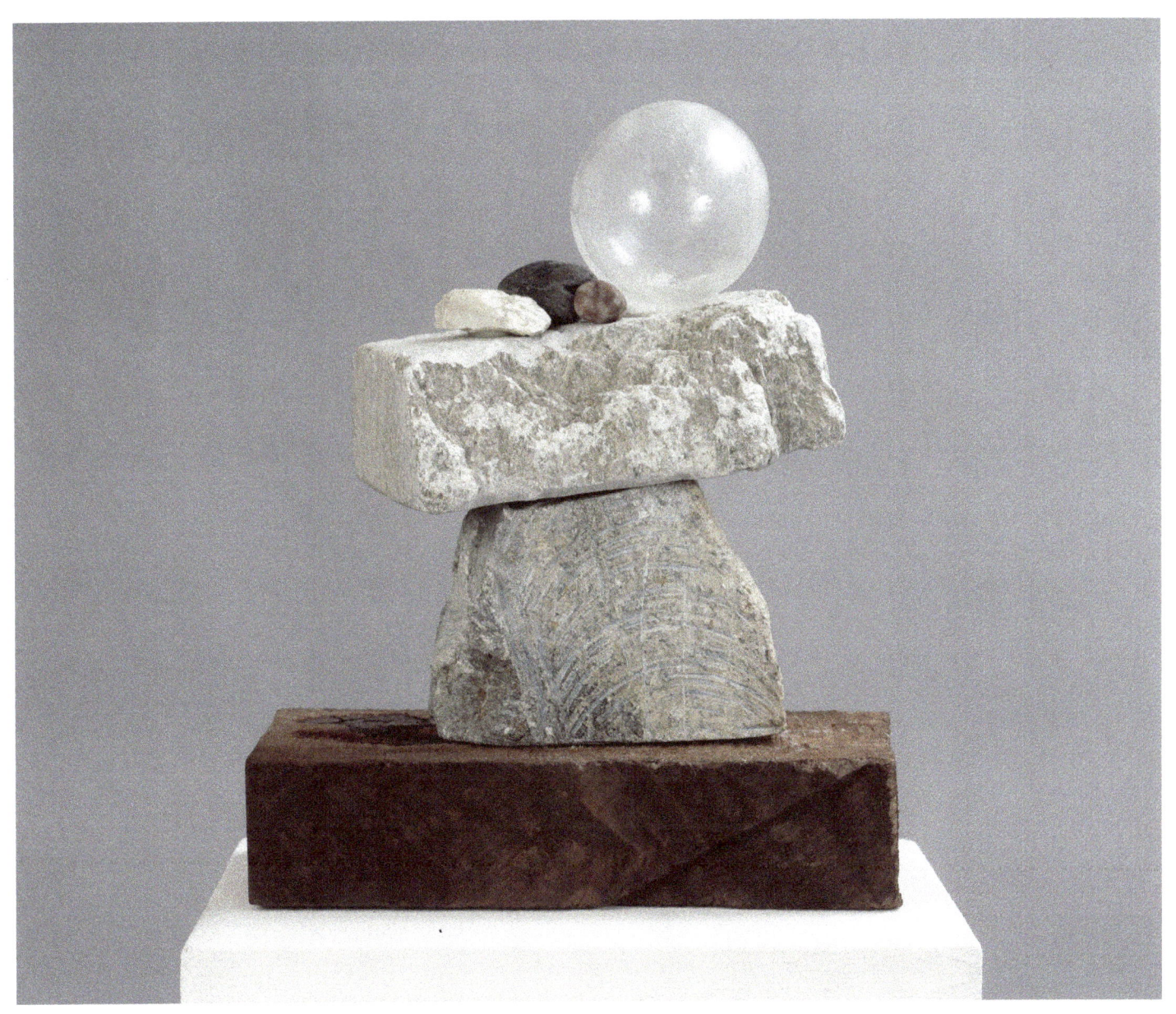

Patricia Bengston-Jones, *A Balanced Moment,* 2011, Redwood, alabaster and glass, 12 x 9 x 7 in.

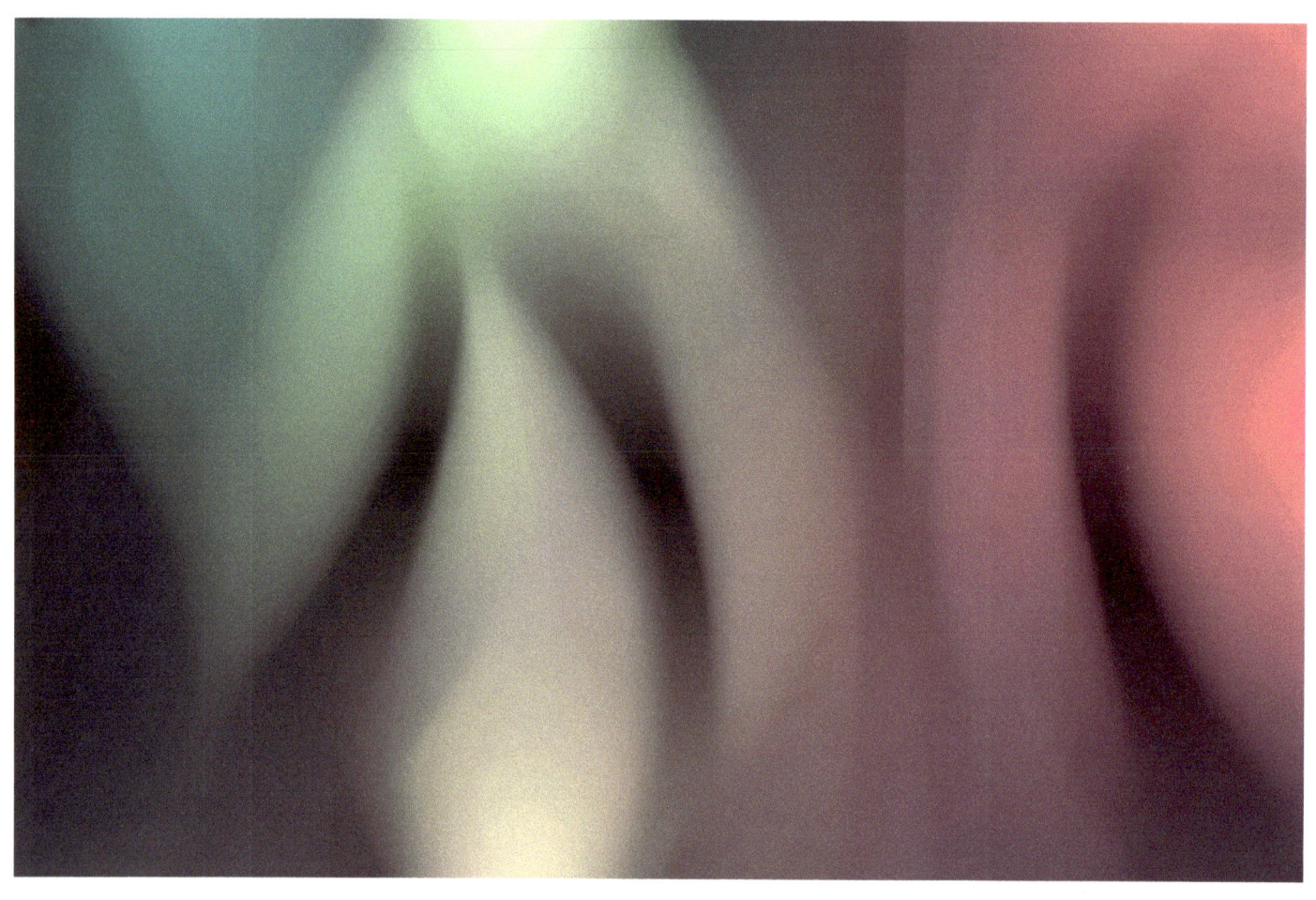

Jeanette Bokhour, *Abstracted Space,* 2006, Ultracrome space

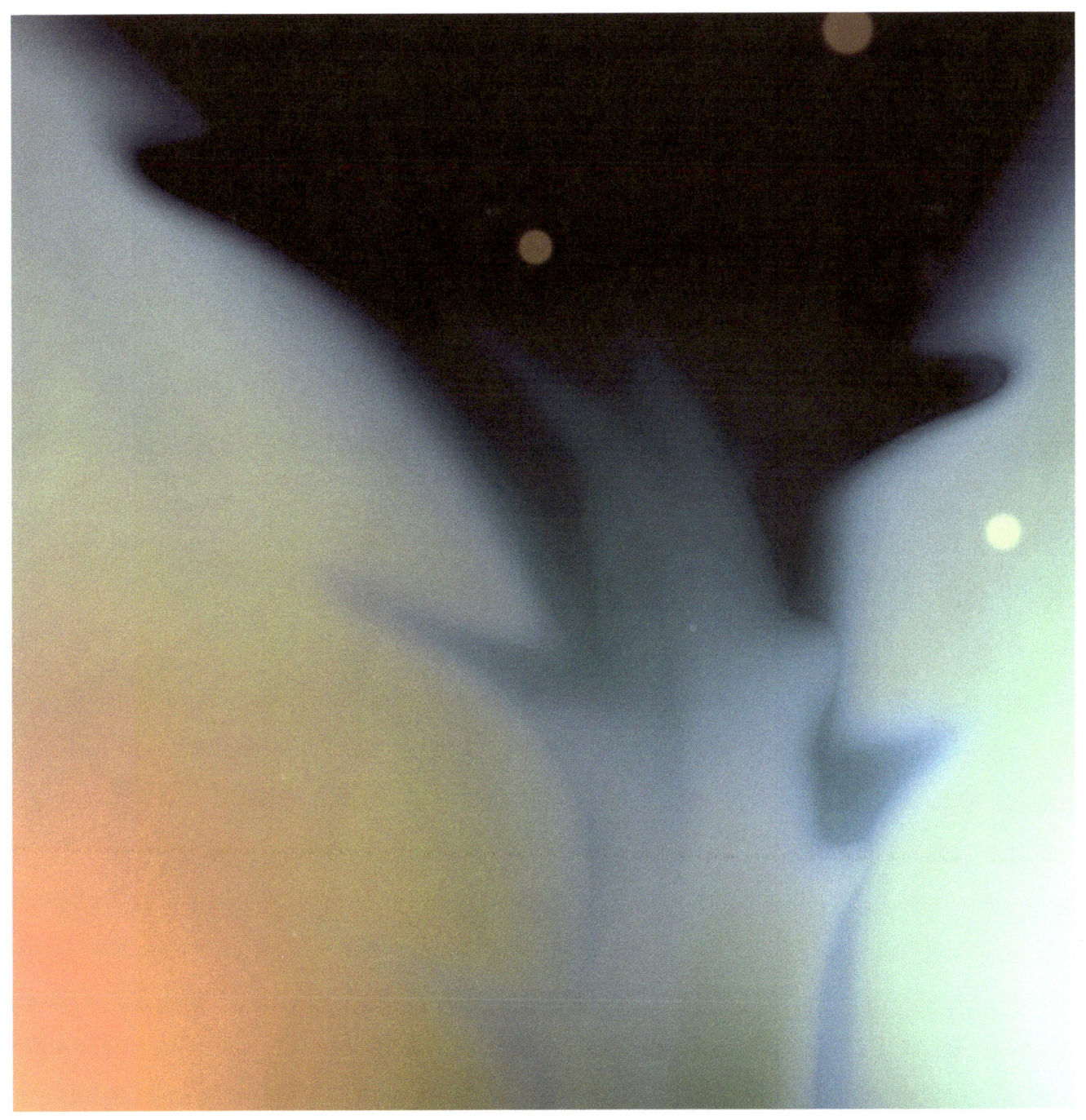

Jeanette Bokhour, *Untitled*, 2006, Ultracrome print

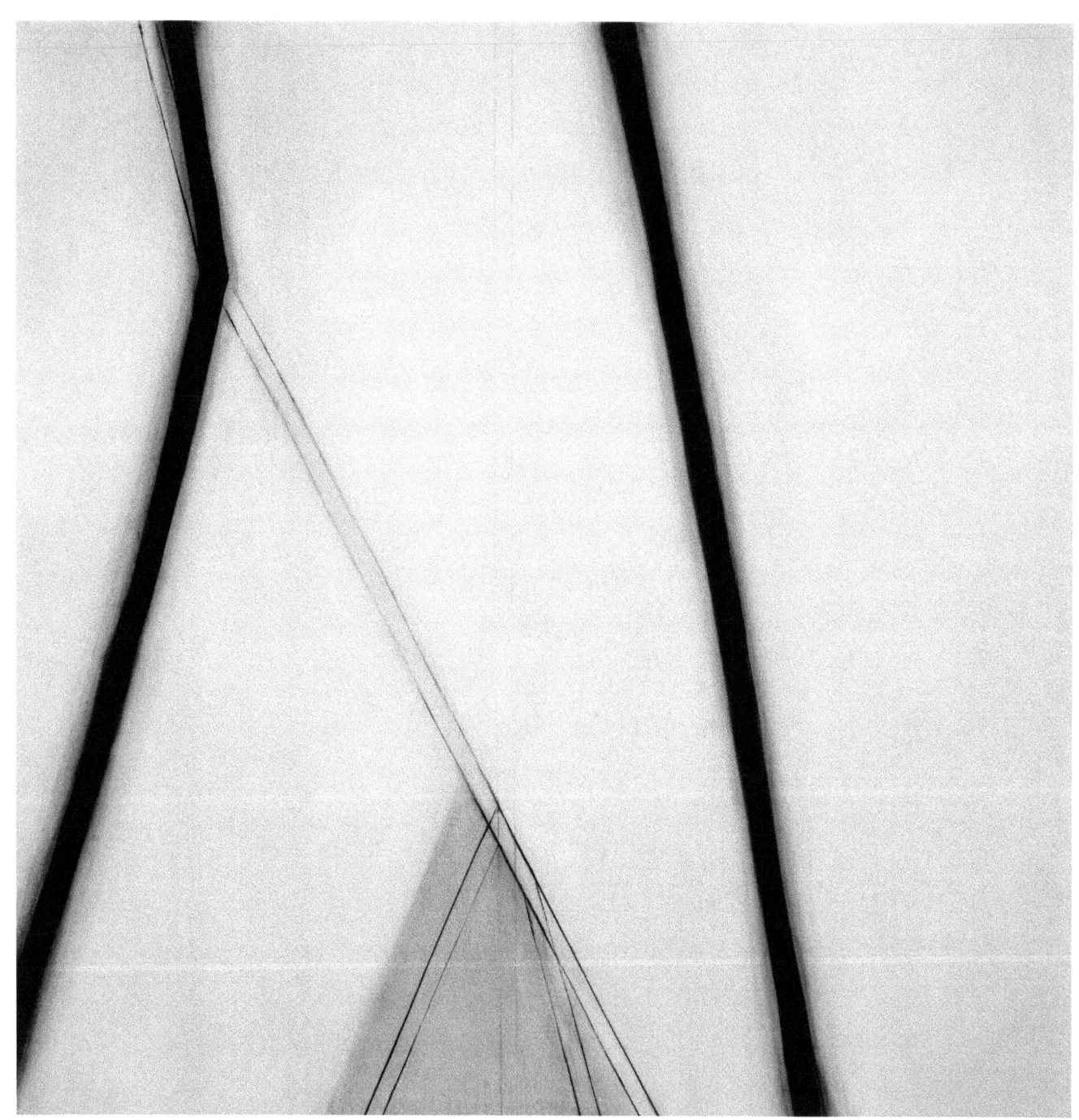

Edythe Bresnahan, *Siena Series #56*, 2008, Oil on panel, 17 x 17 in.

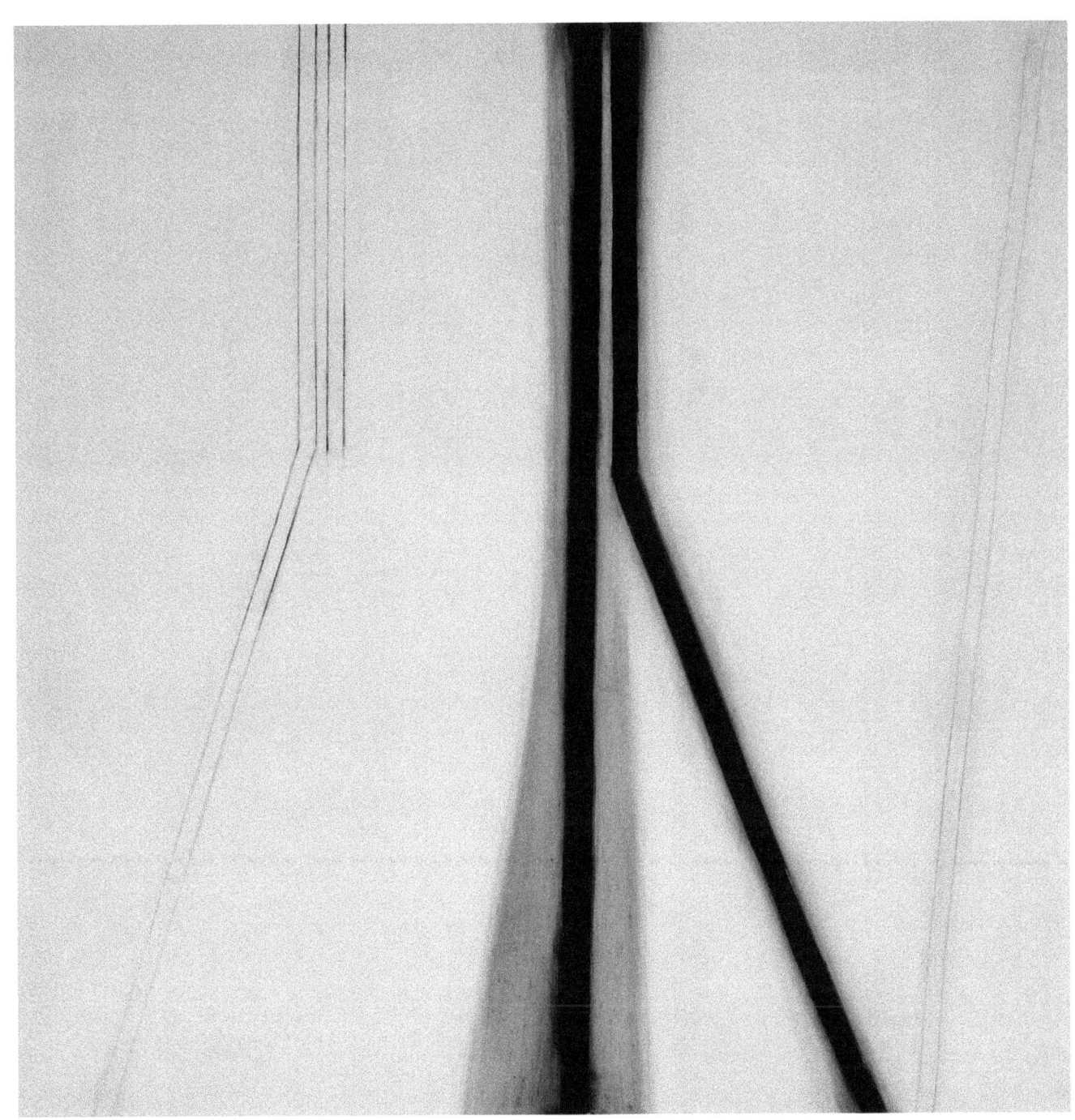

Edythe Bresnahan, *Siena Series #57*, 2008, Oil on panel, 17 x 17 in.

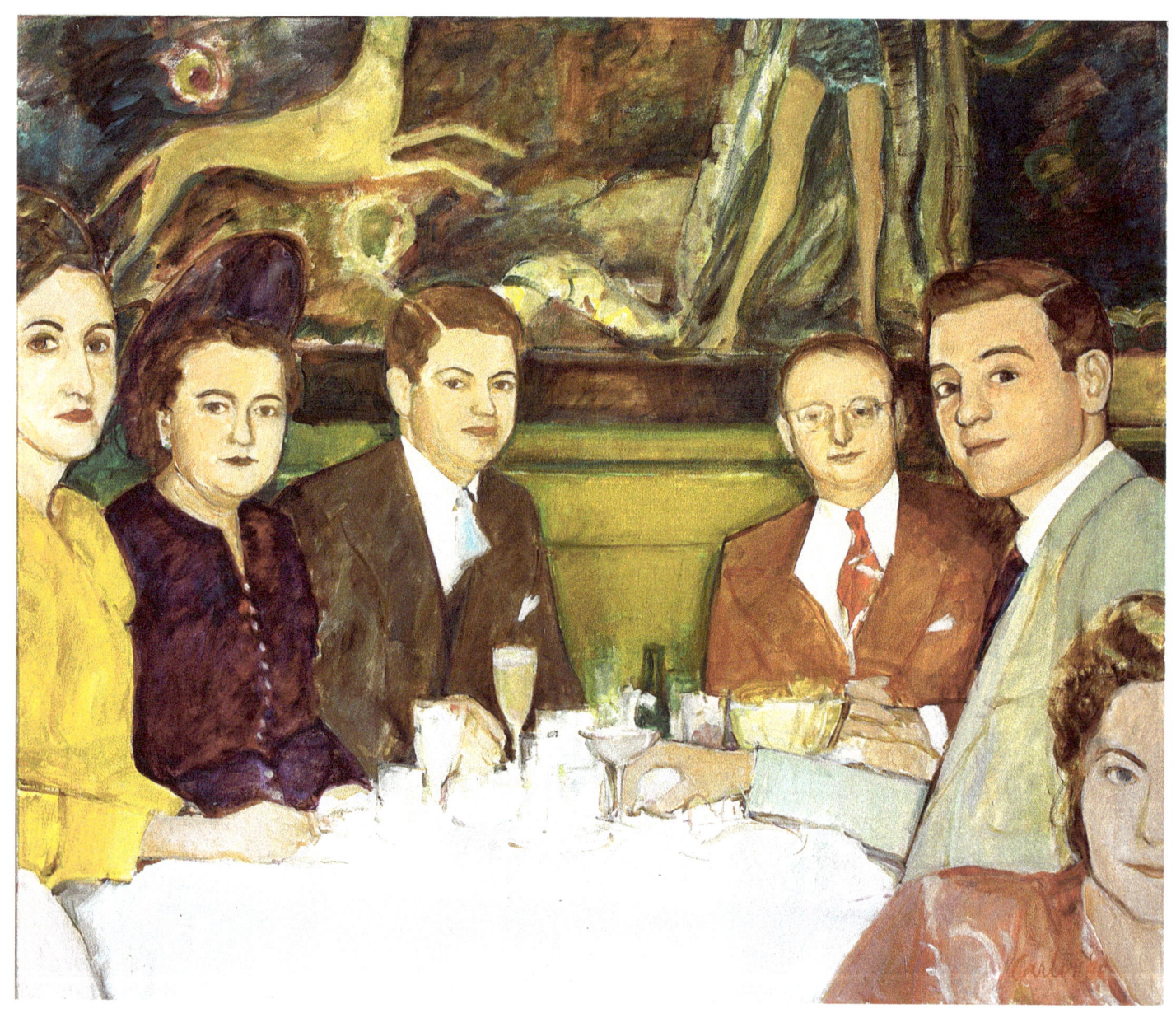

Jerry Carlin, *El Morrocco*, 1986, Oil on canvas, 50 x 60 in.

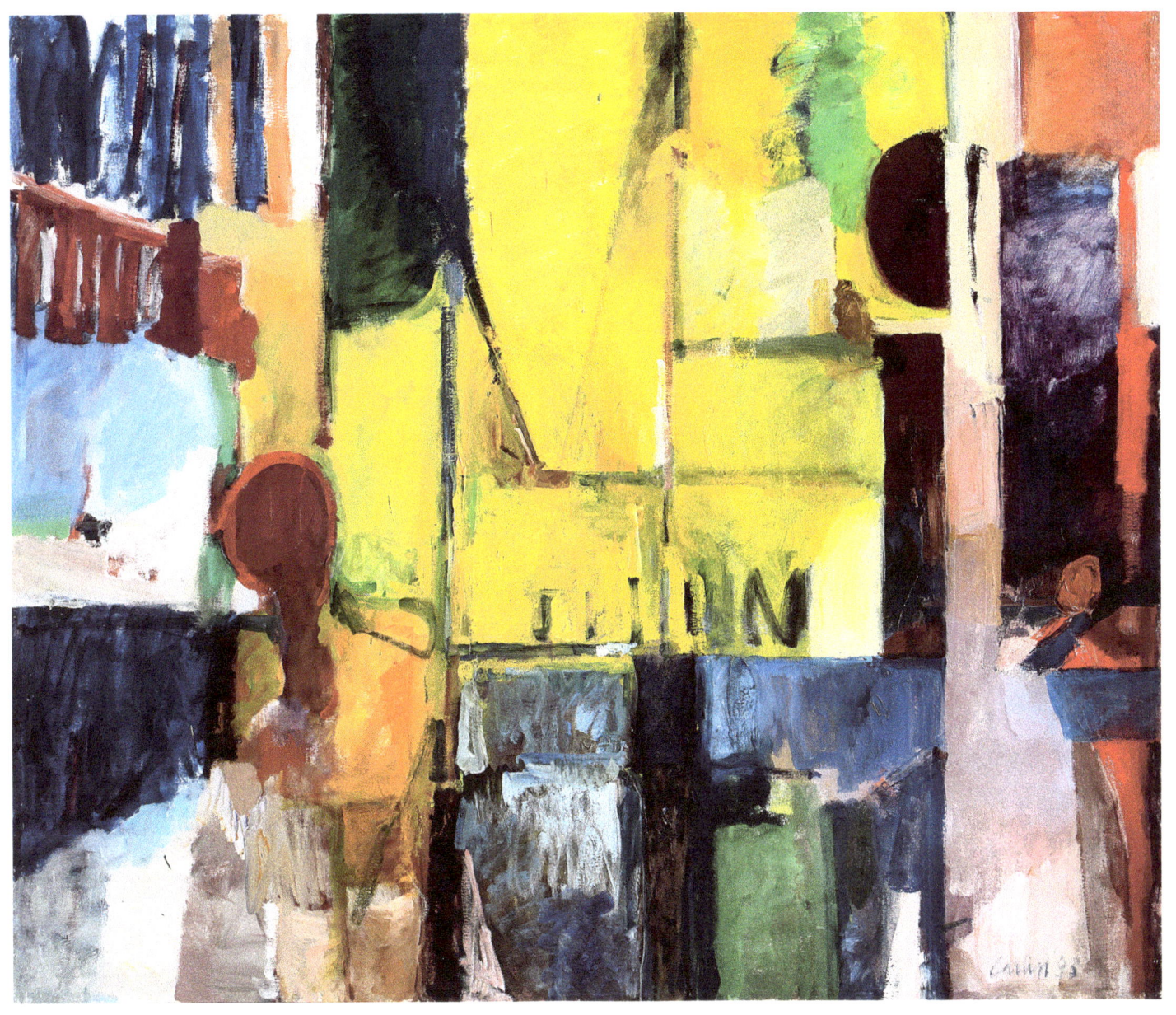

Jerry Carlin, *Pachinko, Tokoyo #2*, 1980-83, Oil on canvas, 60 x 72 in.

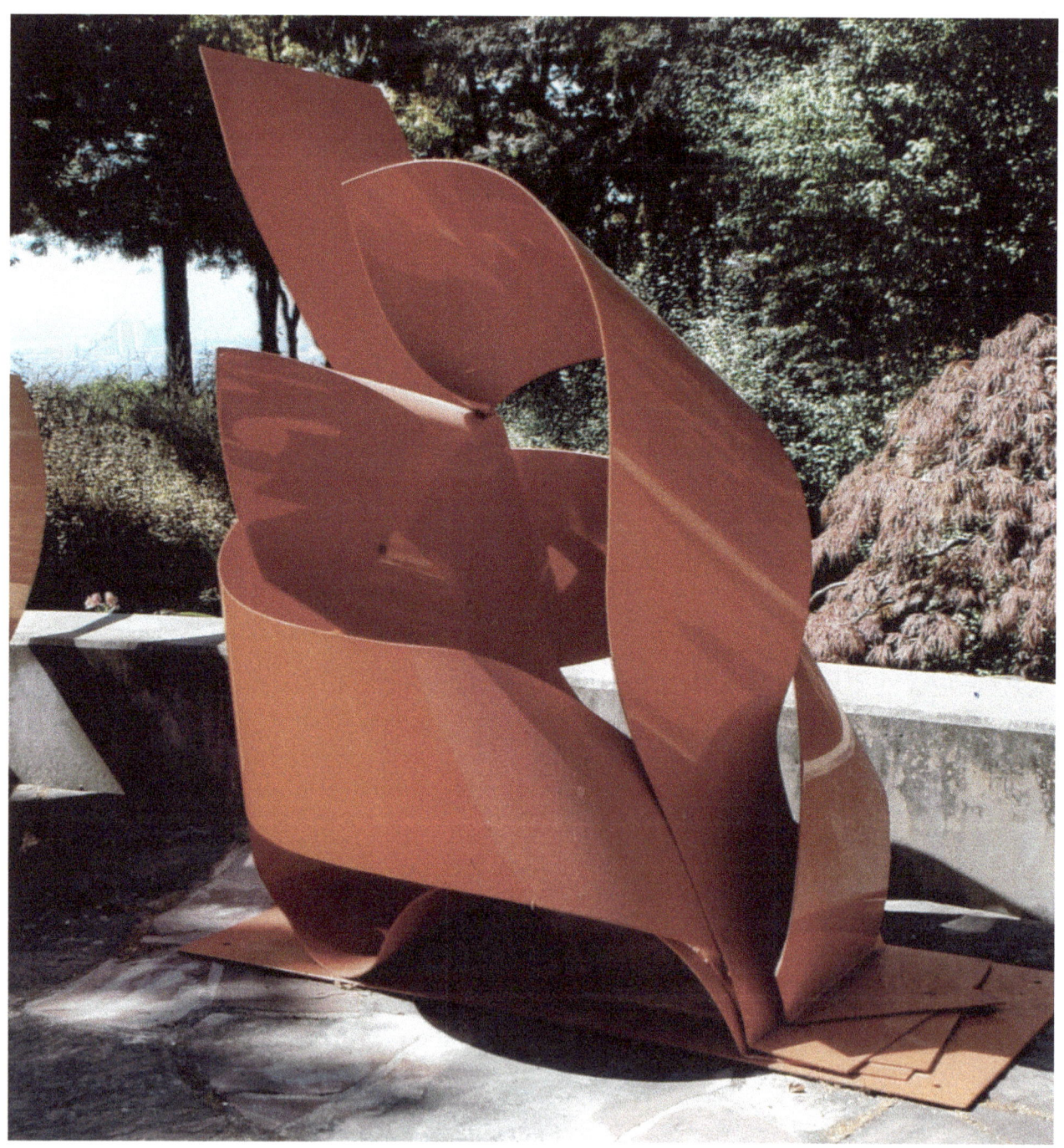

K. Casida, *Flame*, 2010, Painted aluminum and steel, 72 x 71 x 51 in.

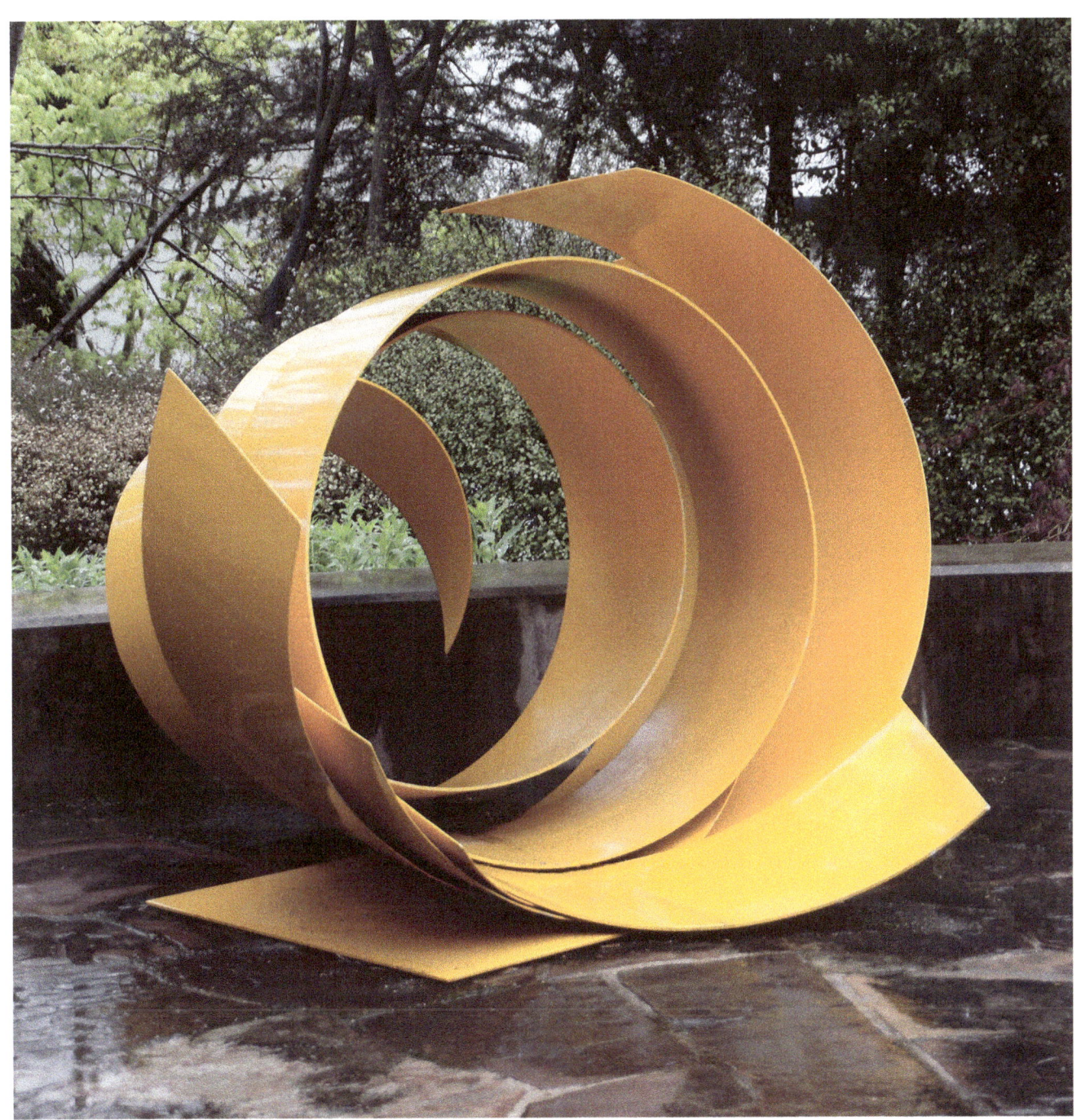

K. Casida, *Pin Curl*, 1994, Painted steel and aluminum, 5 x 12 x 6 ft.

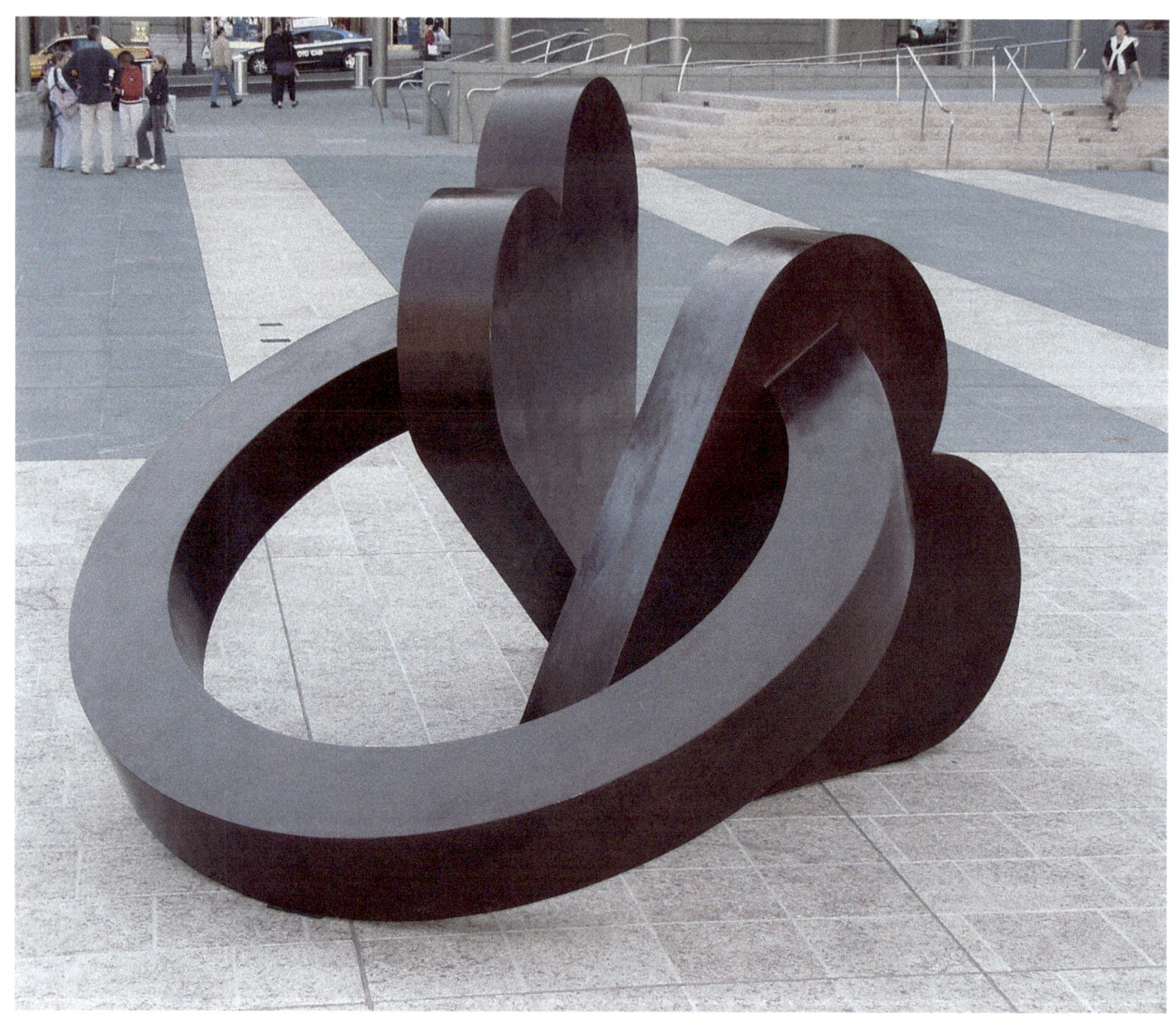

Bruce Chabon, *Link,* 2001, Steel, 120 x 72 x 72 in.

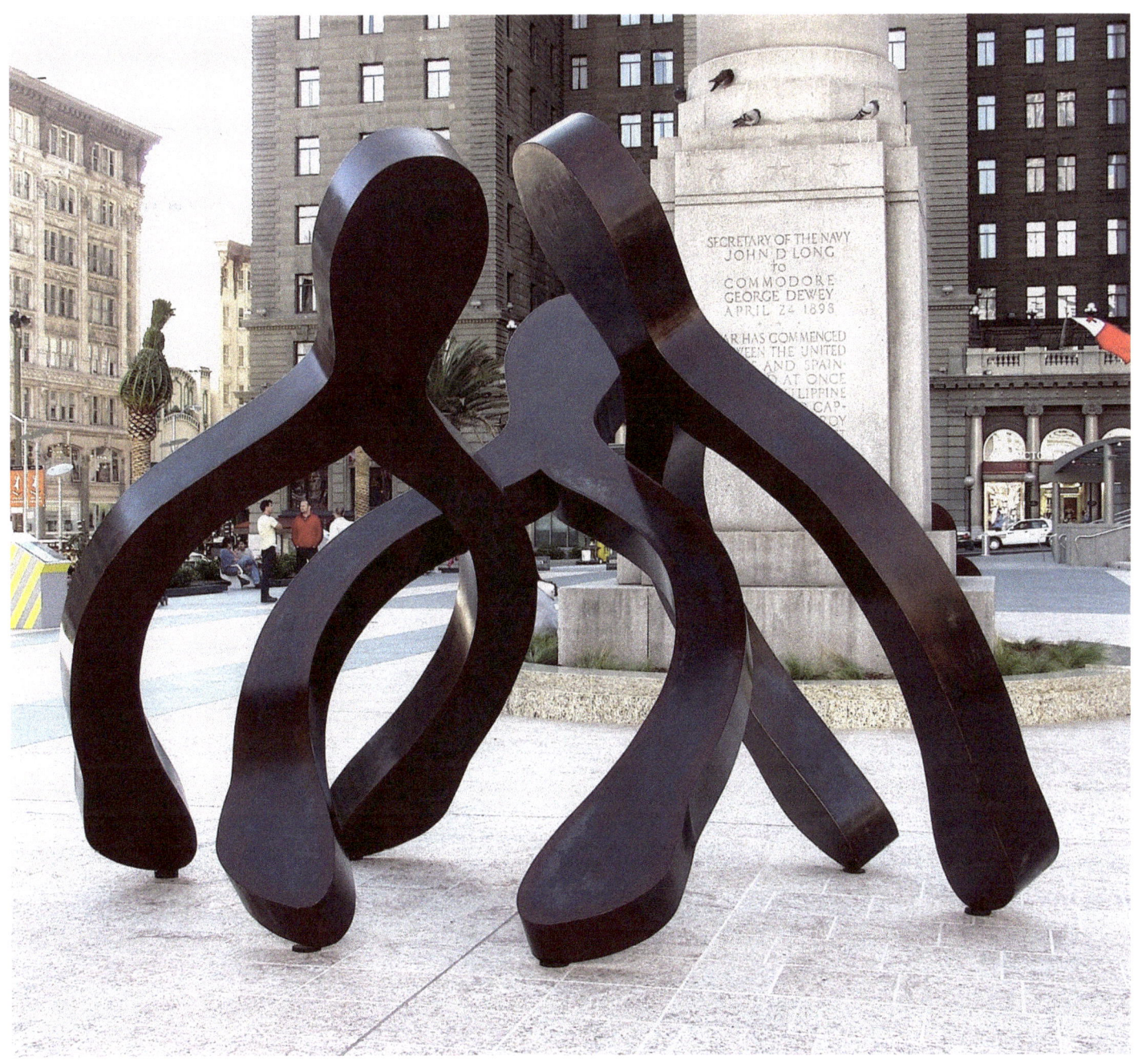

Bruce Chabon, *Three Wishes*, 2001, Steel, 120 x 96 x 72 in.

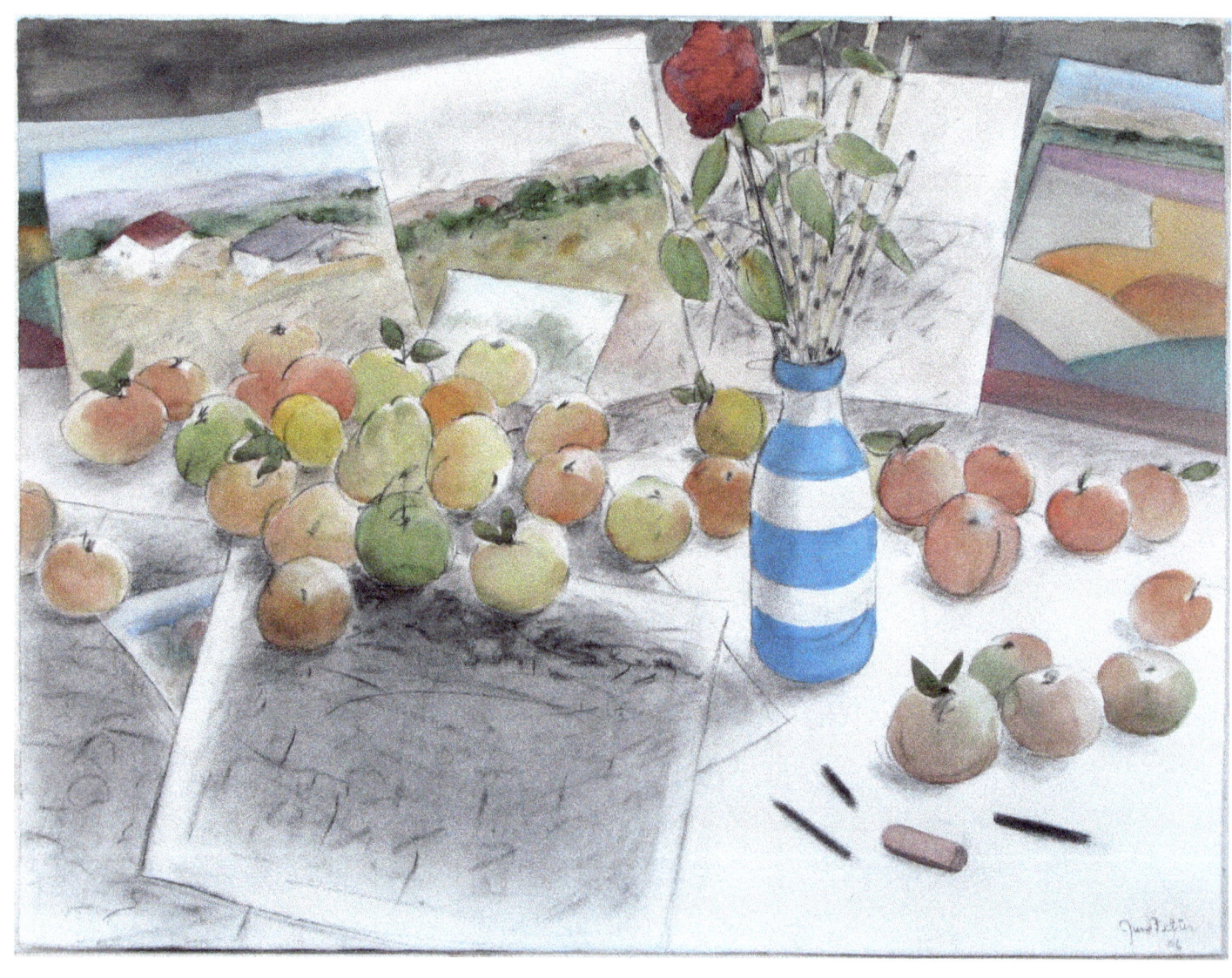

June Felter, *Fruit and Farm Paintings*, 2006, Watercolor, 22 x 30 in.

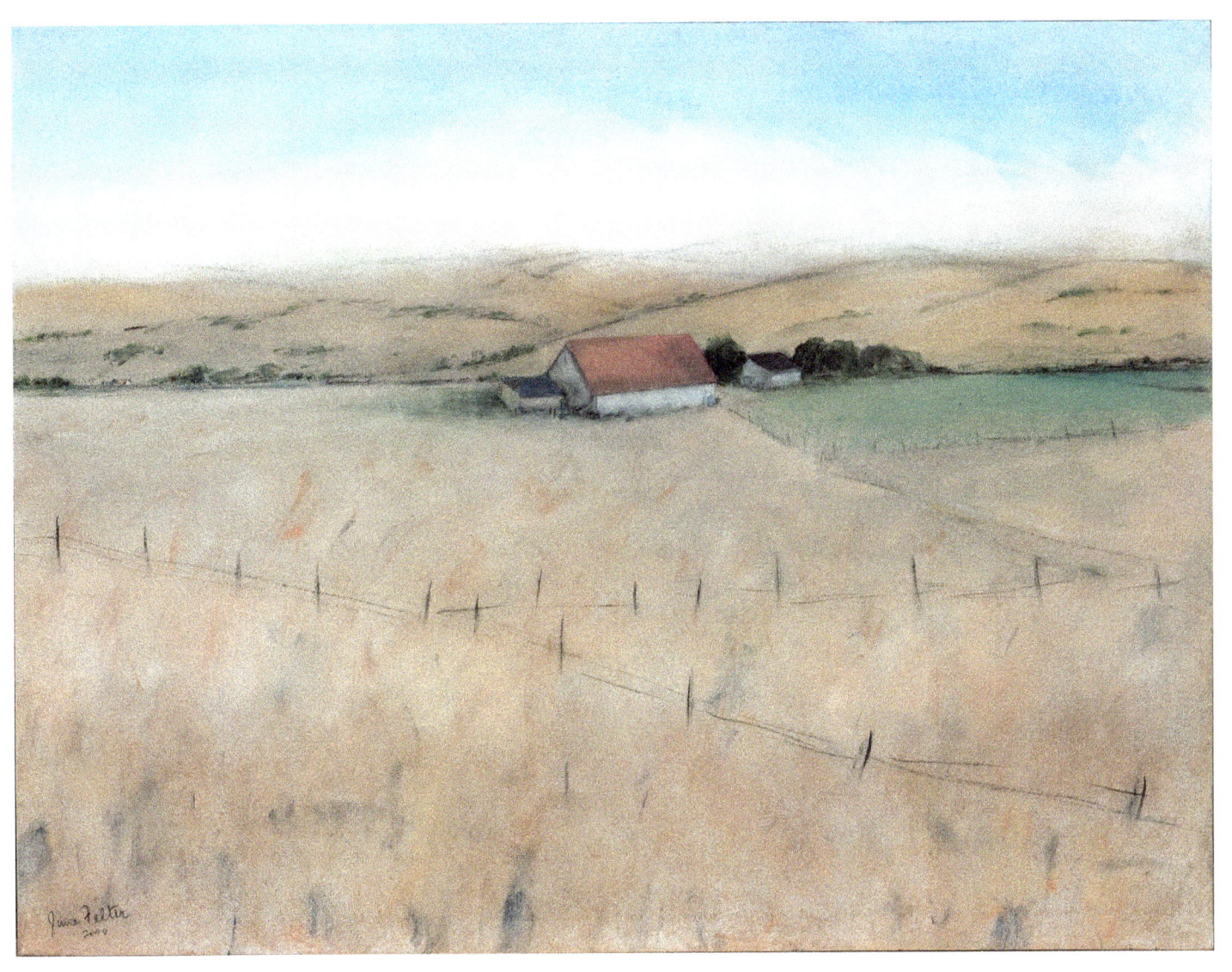

June Felter, *Remembering,* 2009, Acrylic, 36 x 48 in.

Donna Fenstermaker, *Pt. Pinole 12.28.11*, 2011, Oil on canvas, 16 x 12 in.

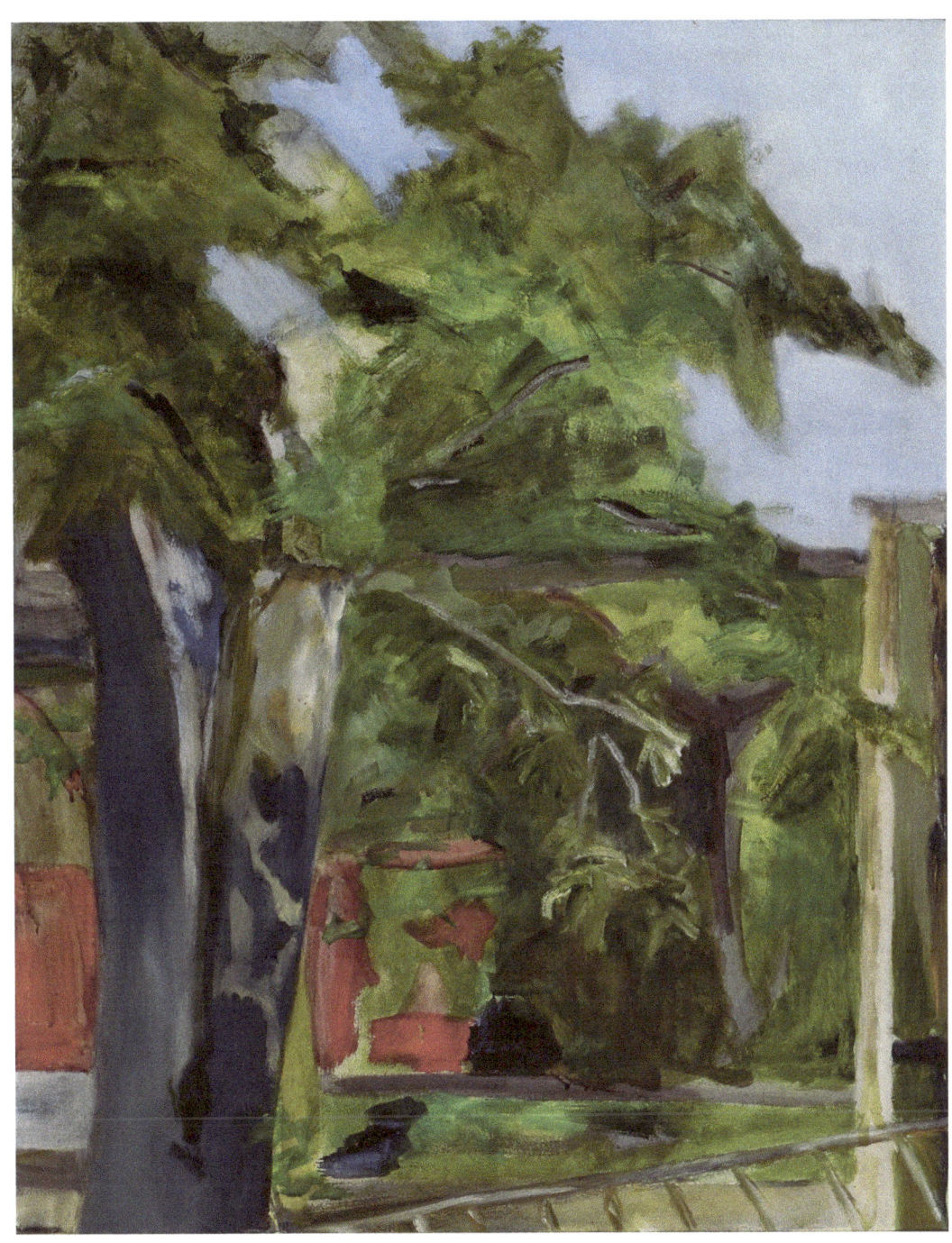

Donna Fenstermaker, *Berkeley Fig 7.19.11*, 2011, Oil on canvas, 30 x 20 in.

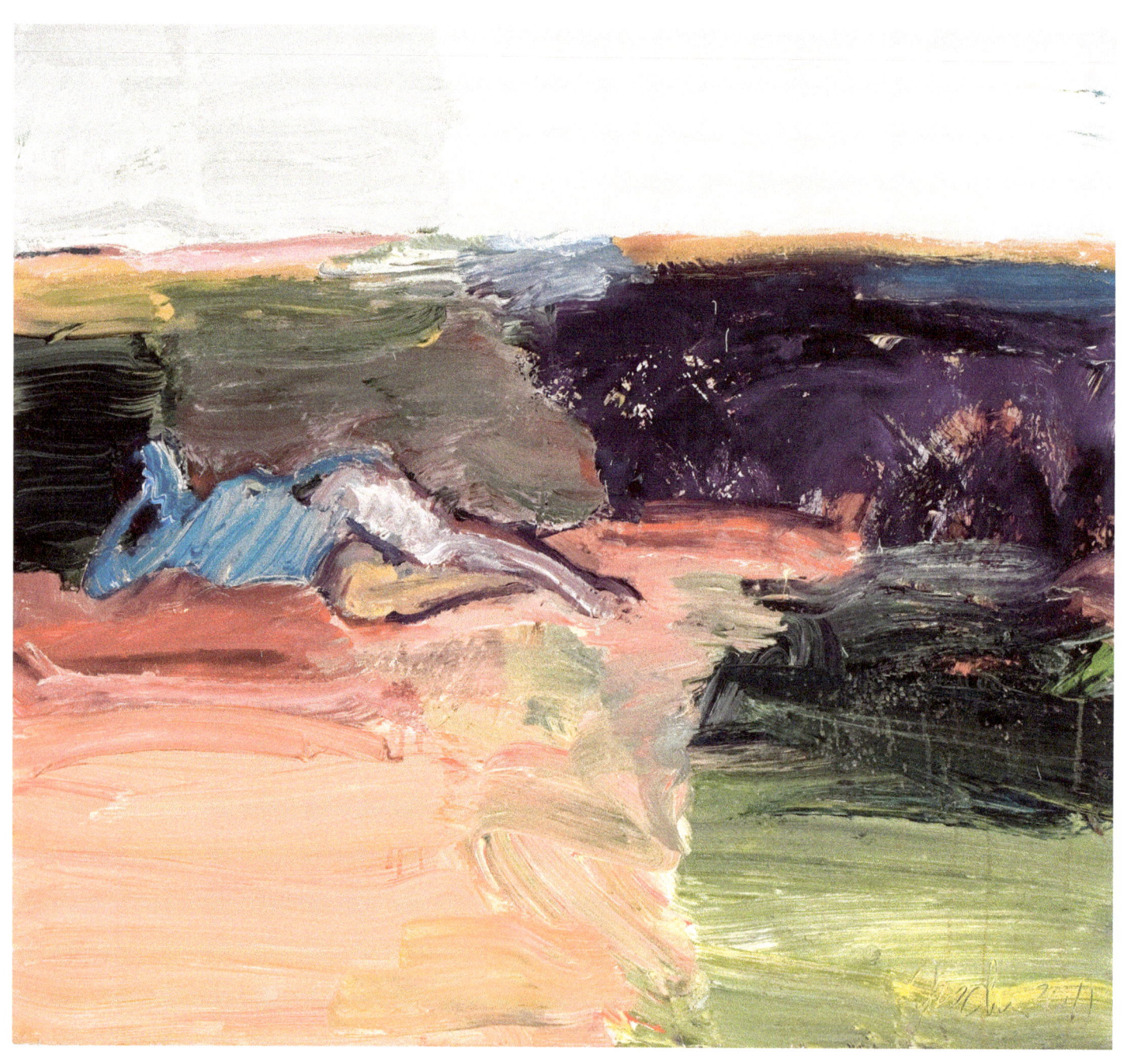

Lin Fischer, *Blue Torso*, 2011, Acrylic on canvas, 36 x 40 in.

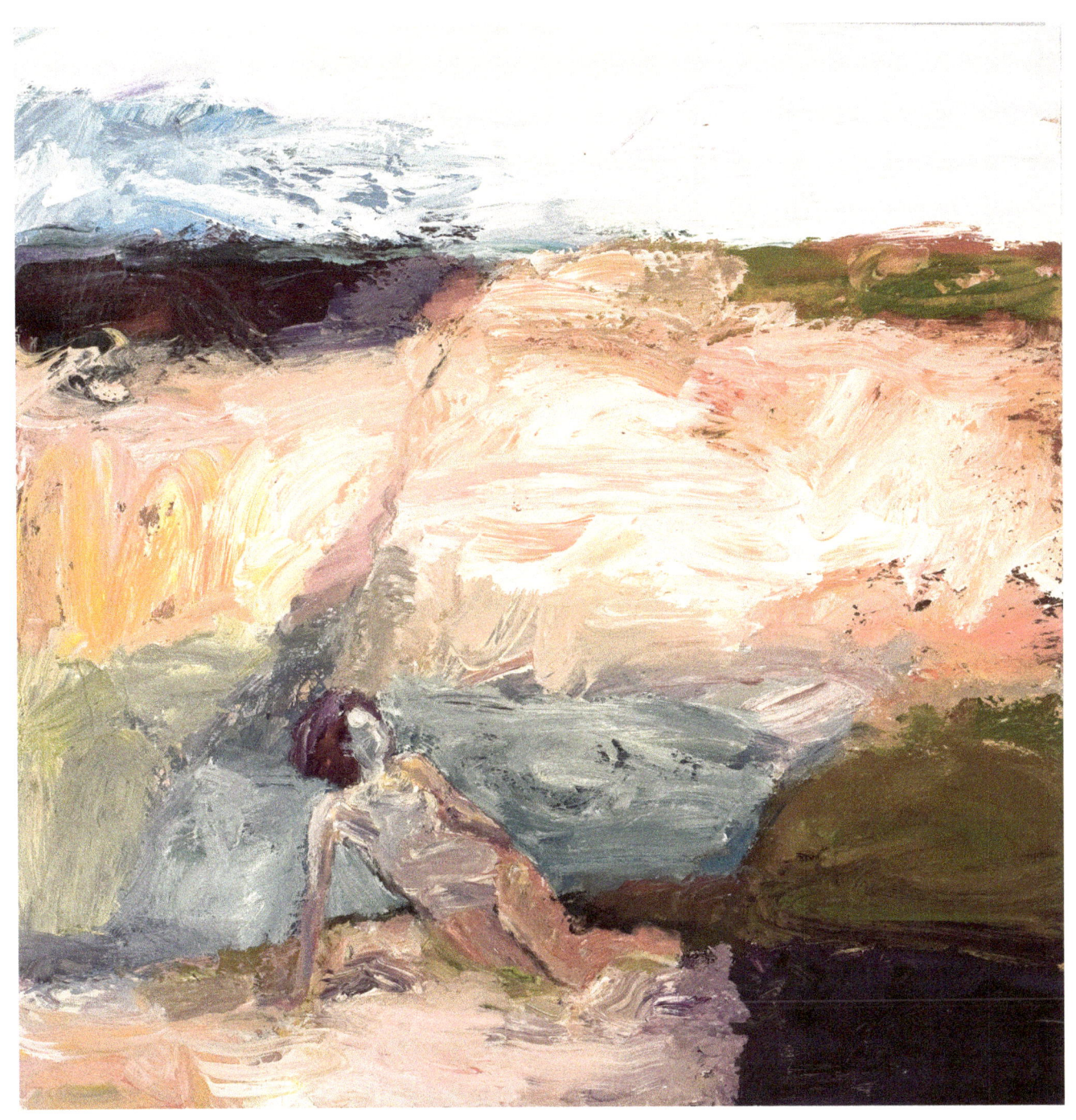

Lin Fischer, *Near Water*, 2011, Acrylic on canvas, 48 x 48 in.

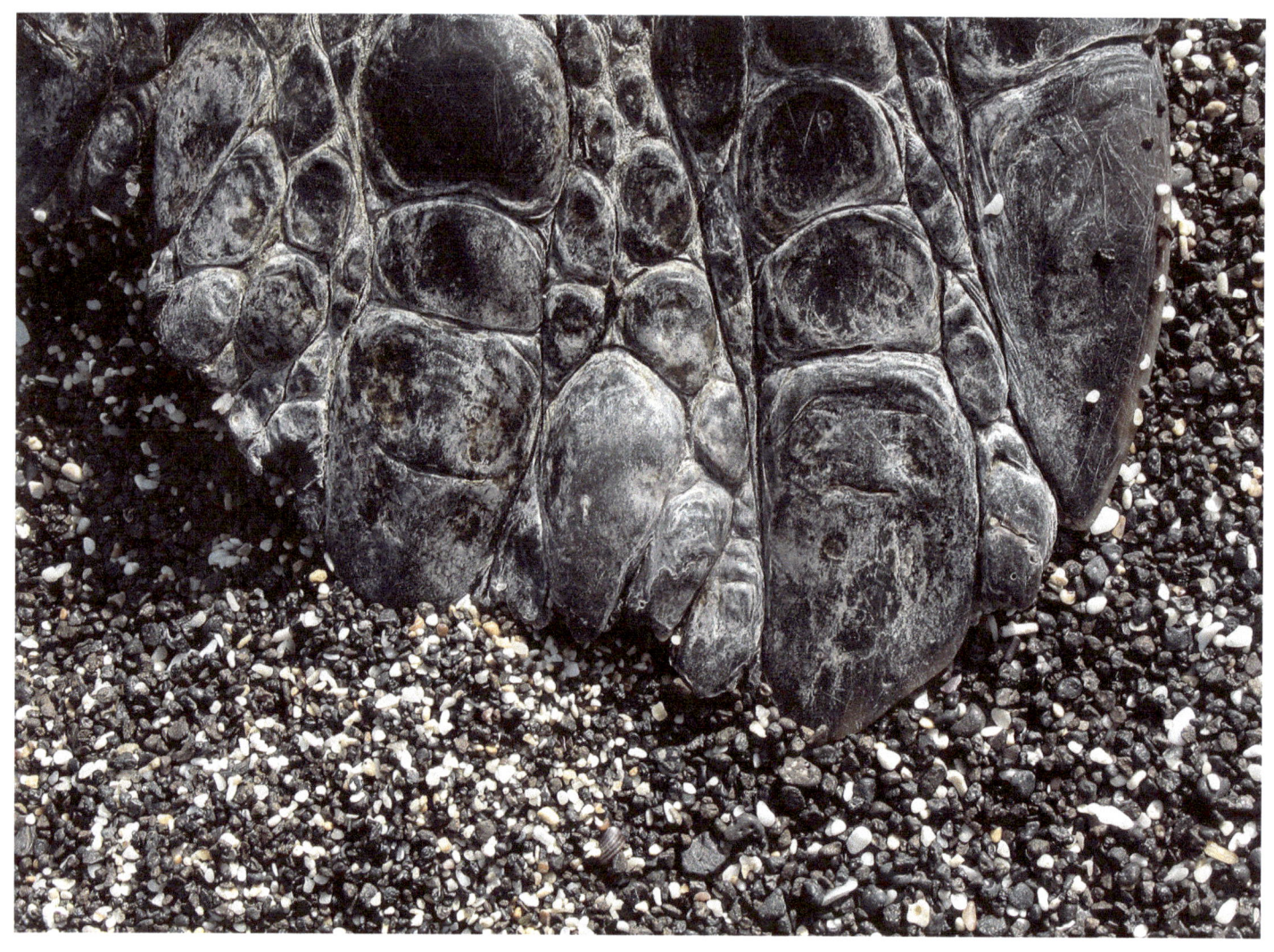

John Friedman, *Beach and Sea Turtle Hawaii Island*, 2008, Photograph

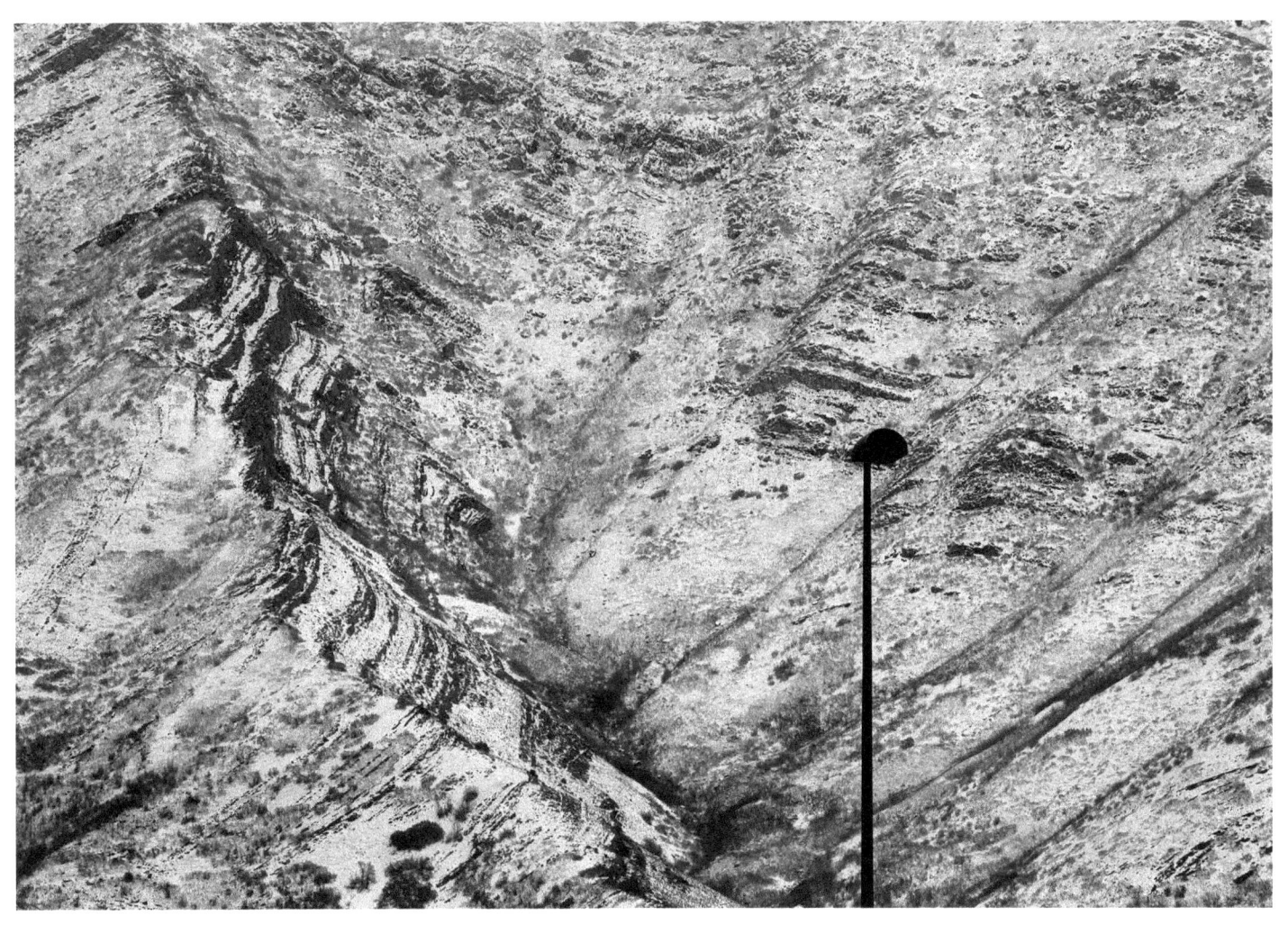

John Friedman, *Truck Stop and Oquirrh Range Toolee-Lake Point, Utah*, 2011 Photograph

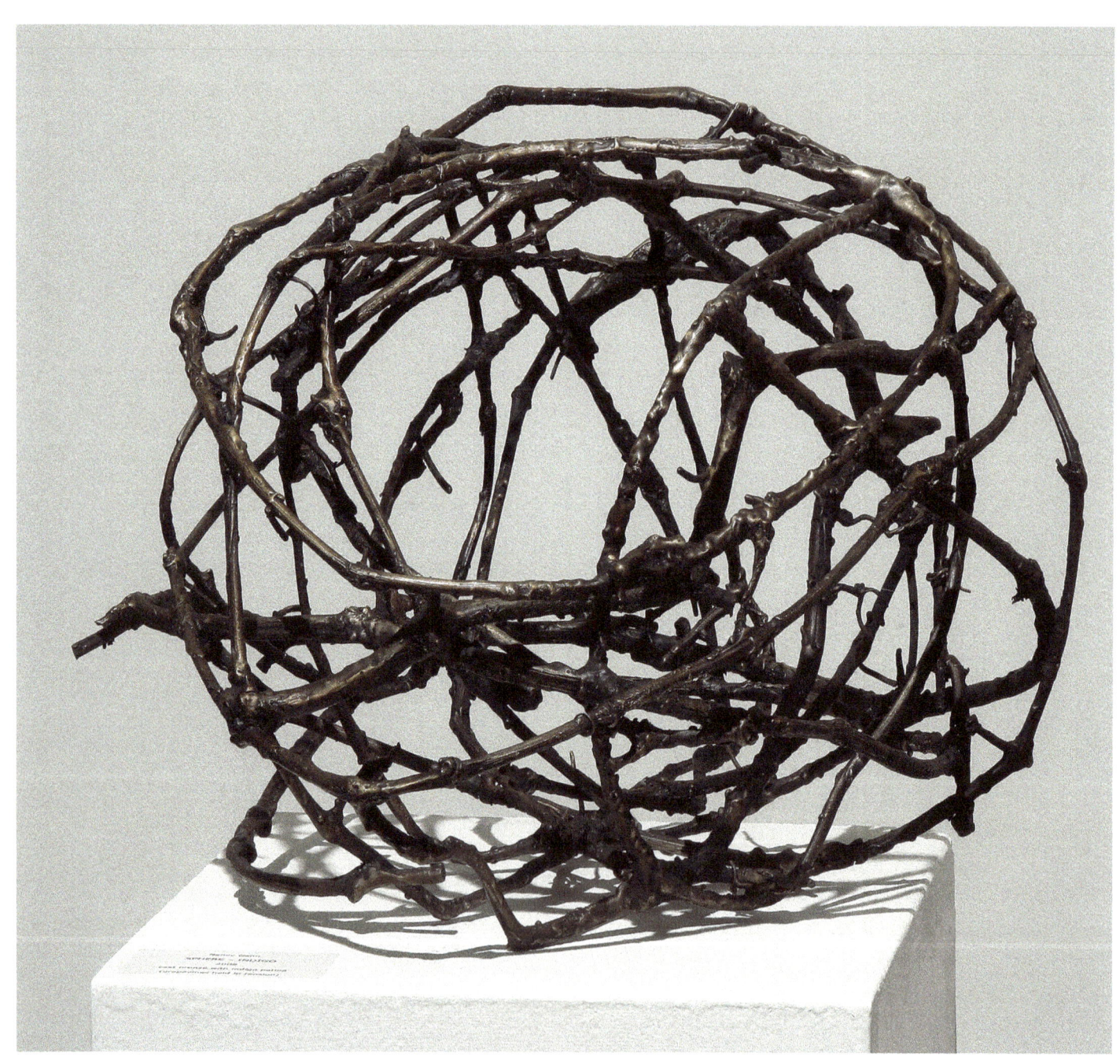

Nancy Genn, *Pacifica ll*, 2011, Cast bronze, 12 x 19x 17 in.

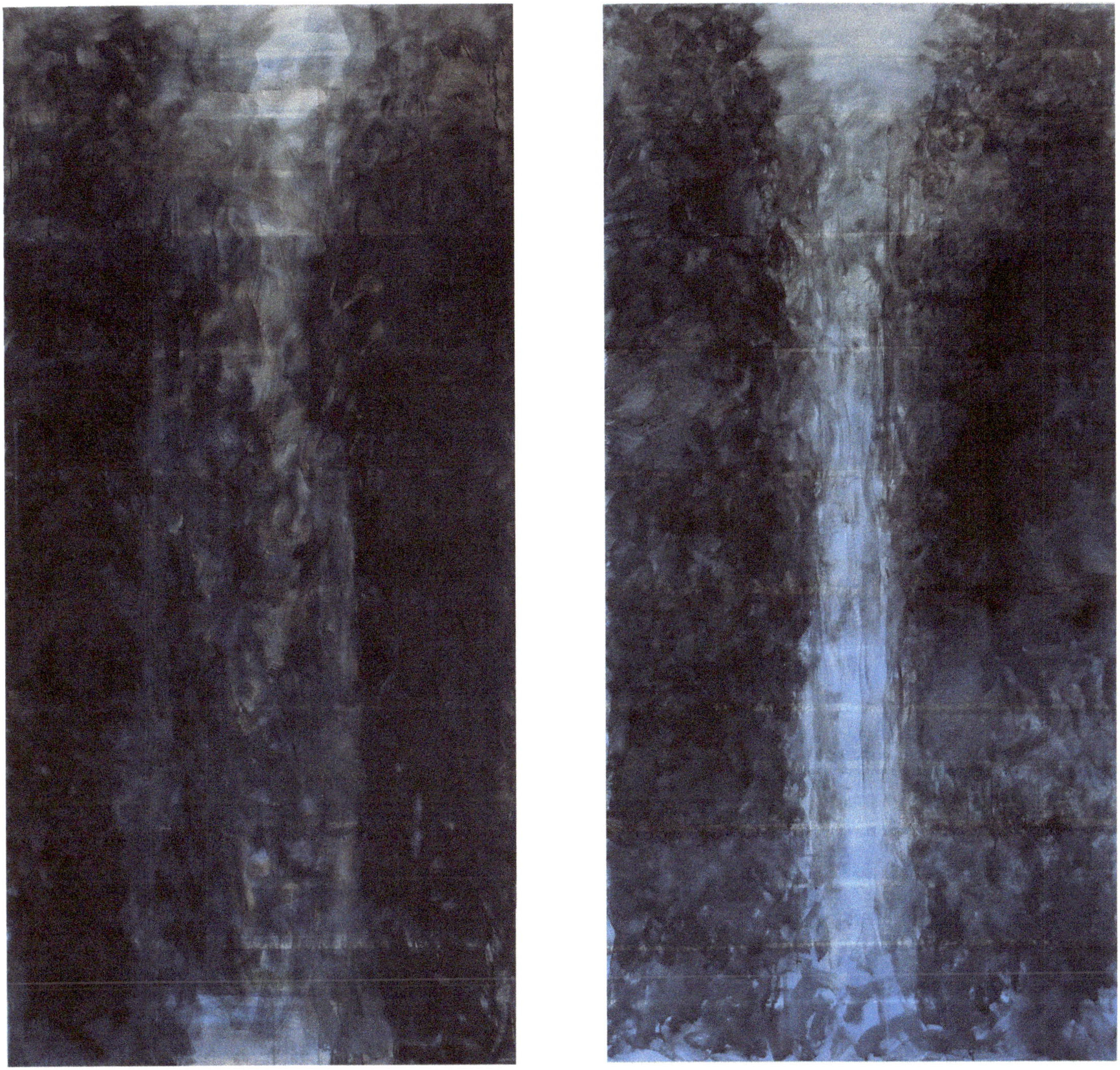

Nancy Genn, *Waterfall Change is Eternal I and Change is Eternal II*, 2011, Casein on canvas, 72 x 30 in. each

Katie Hawkinson, *Radiate*, 2011, Oil on linen, 48 x 48 in.

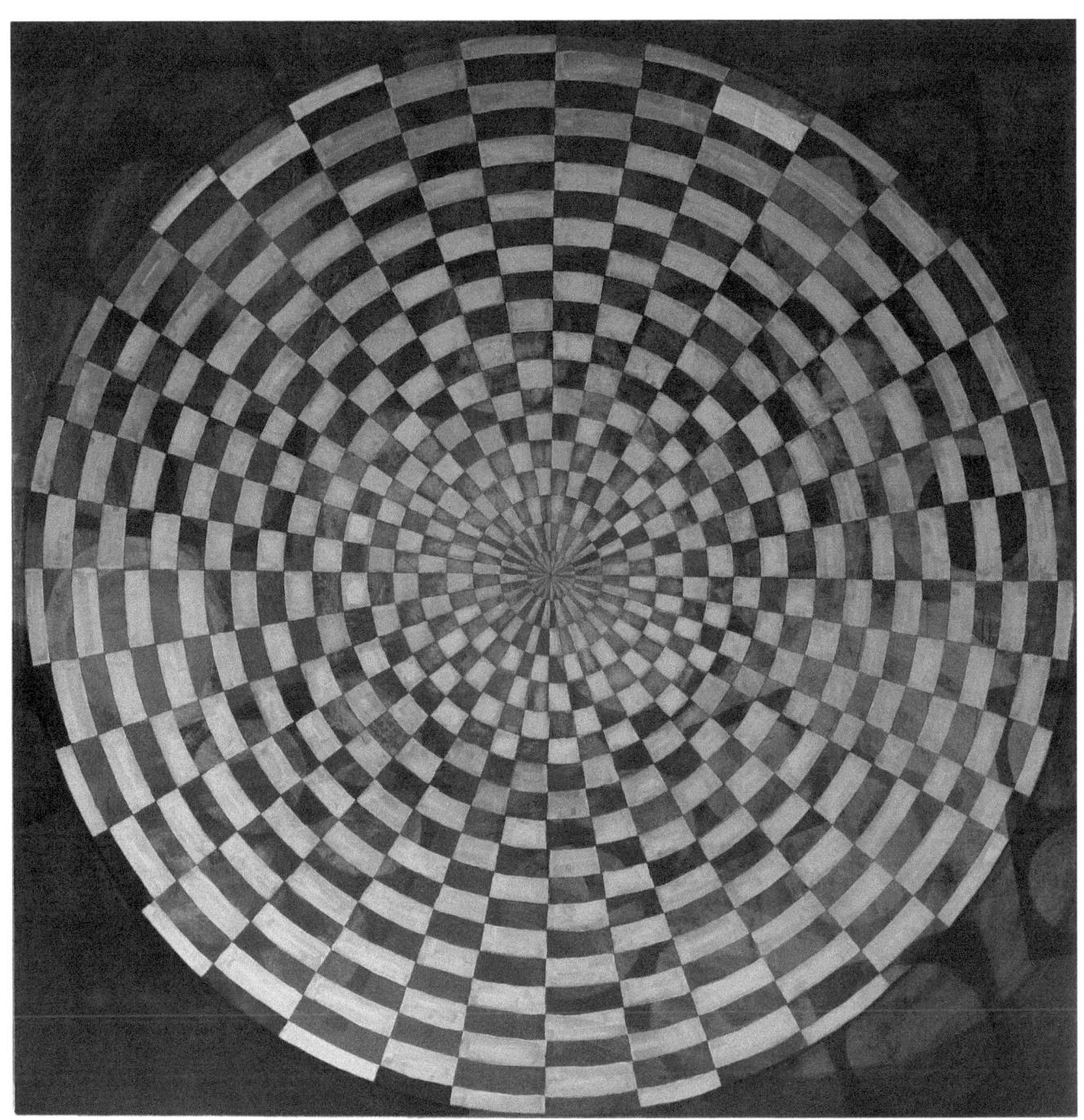

Katie Hawkinson, *Pulsation of the Universe*, 2012, Oil on linen, 60 x 60 in.

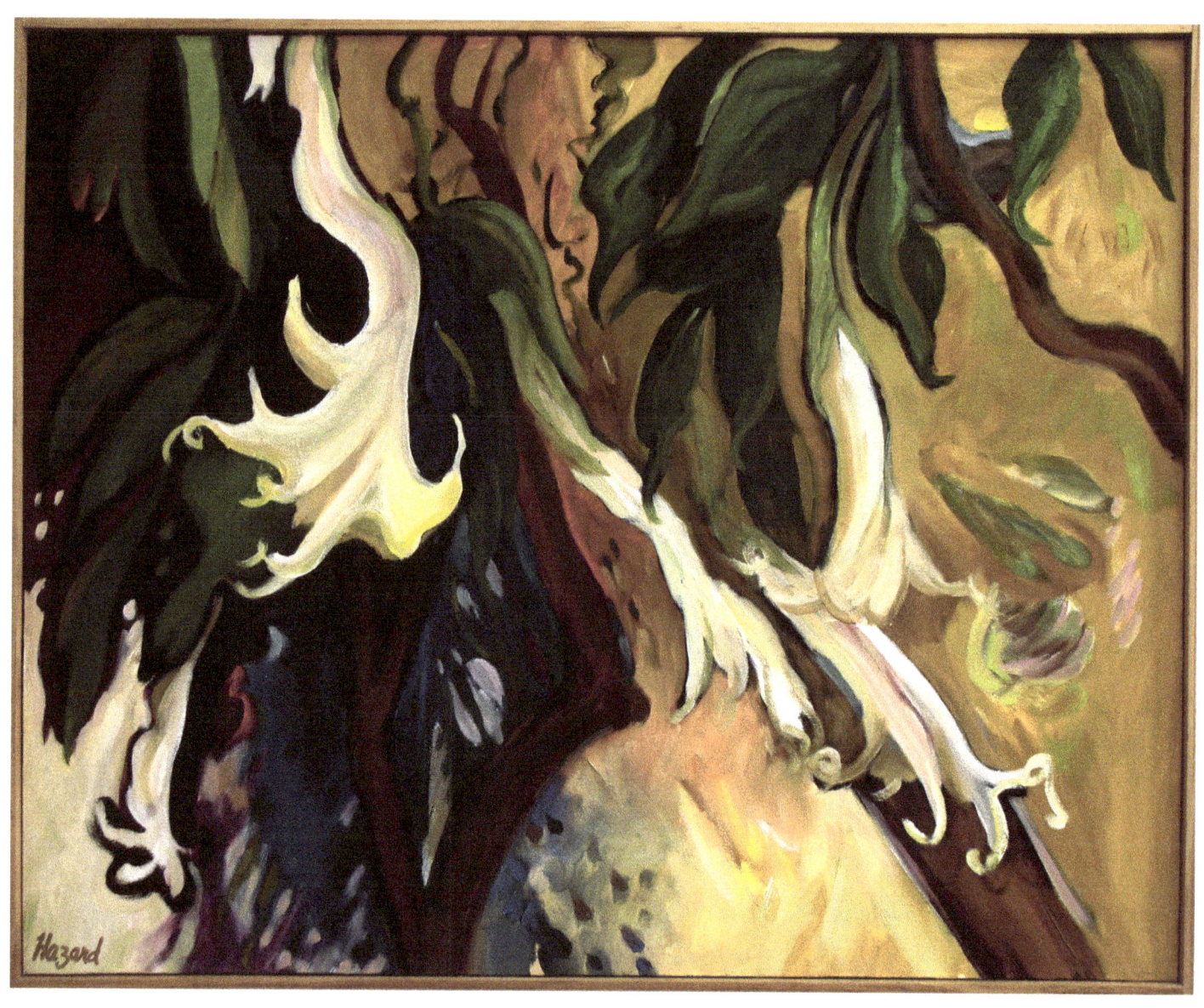

Barbara Hazard, *Angel Trumpet 2007*, 2007, Oil on canvas, 22 x 28 in.

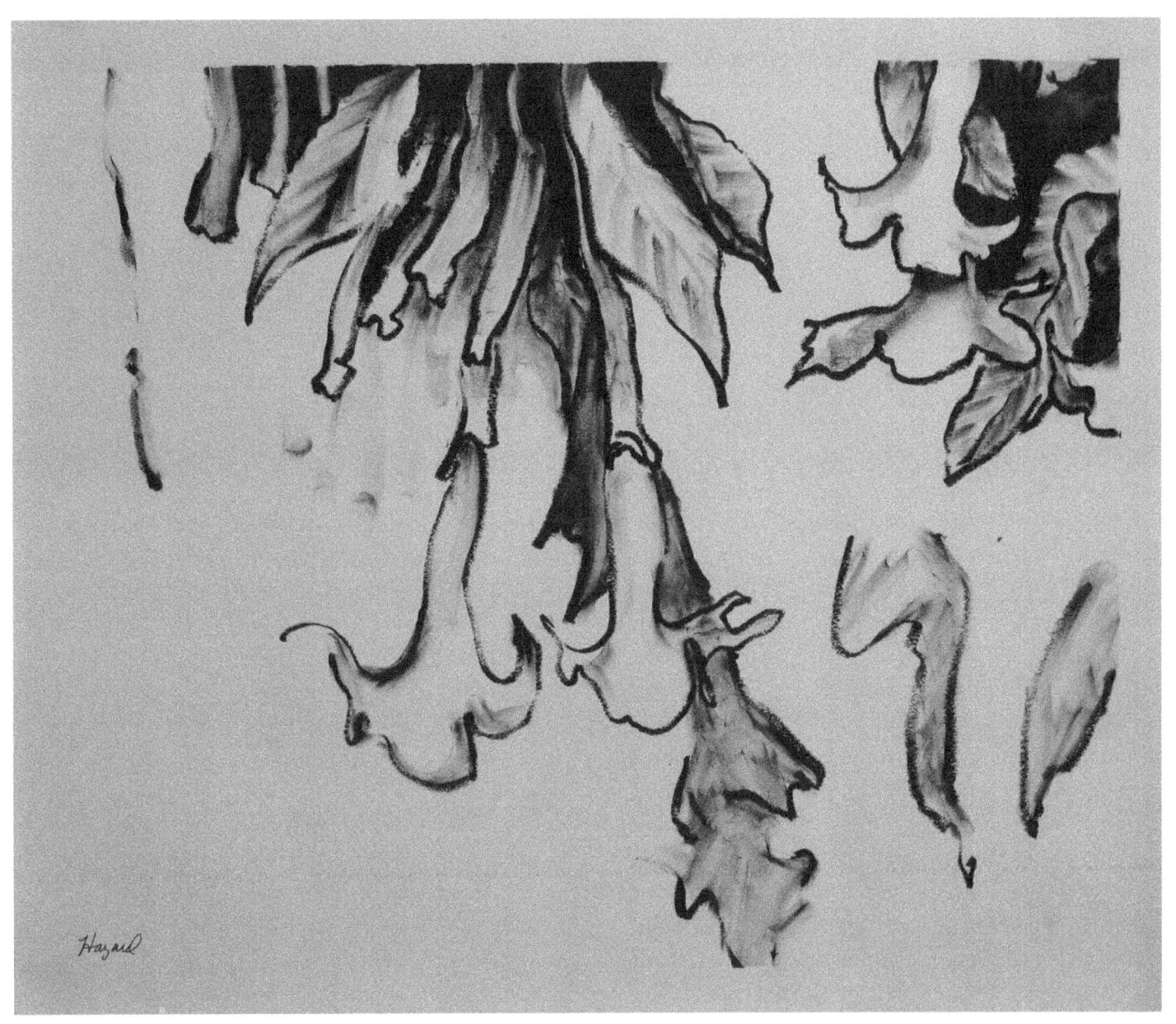

Barbara Hazard, *Angel Trumpet 2008*, 2008, Oil stick on paper, 20 x 23 in.

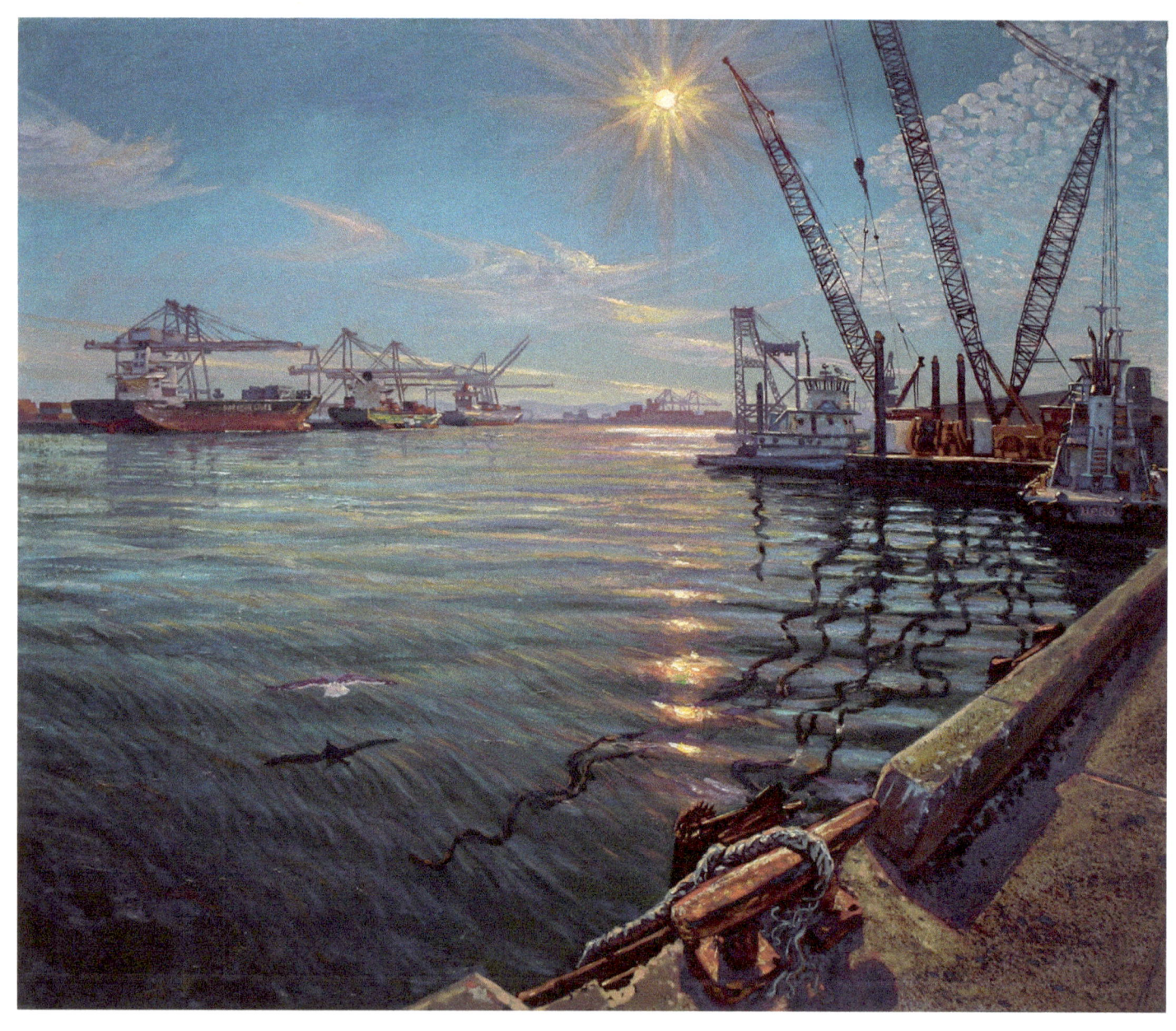

Anthony Holdsworth, *Winter Sun, Port of Oakland*, 2011, Oil on canvas, 34 x 40 in.

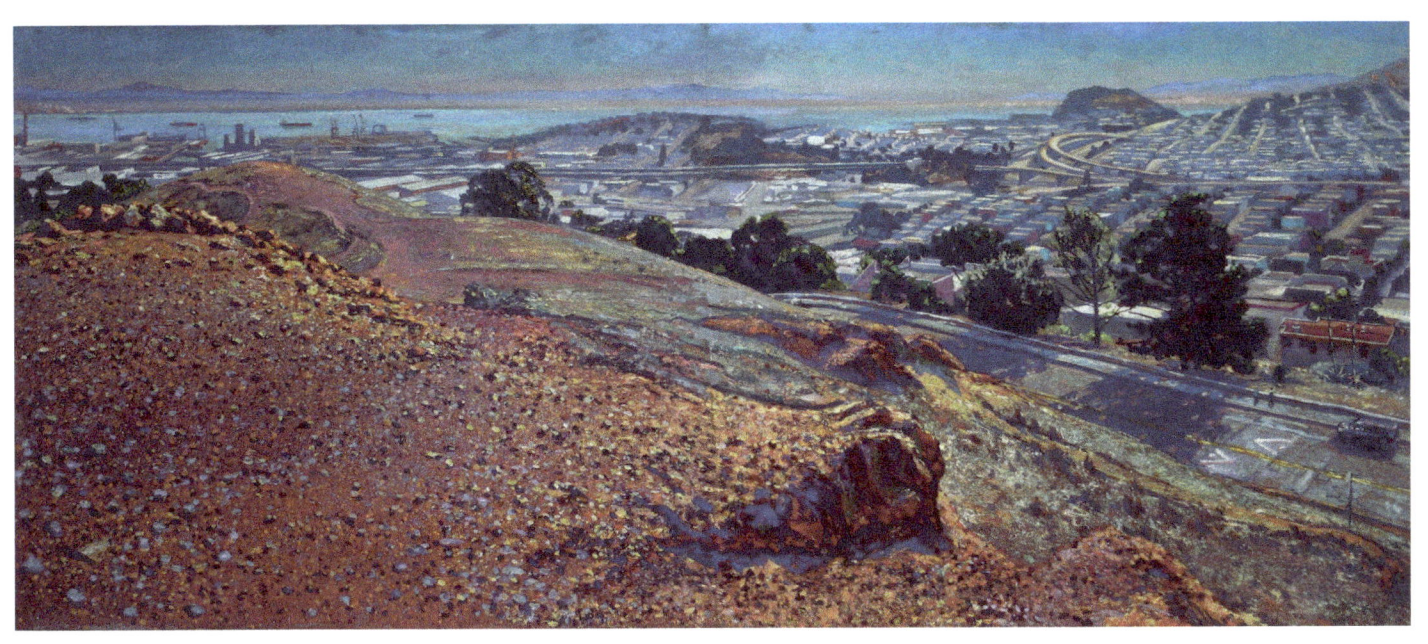

Anthony Holdsworth, *Bernal Hill Series #5*, 2010, Oil on hardwood plywood, 24 x 48 in.

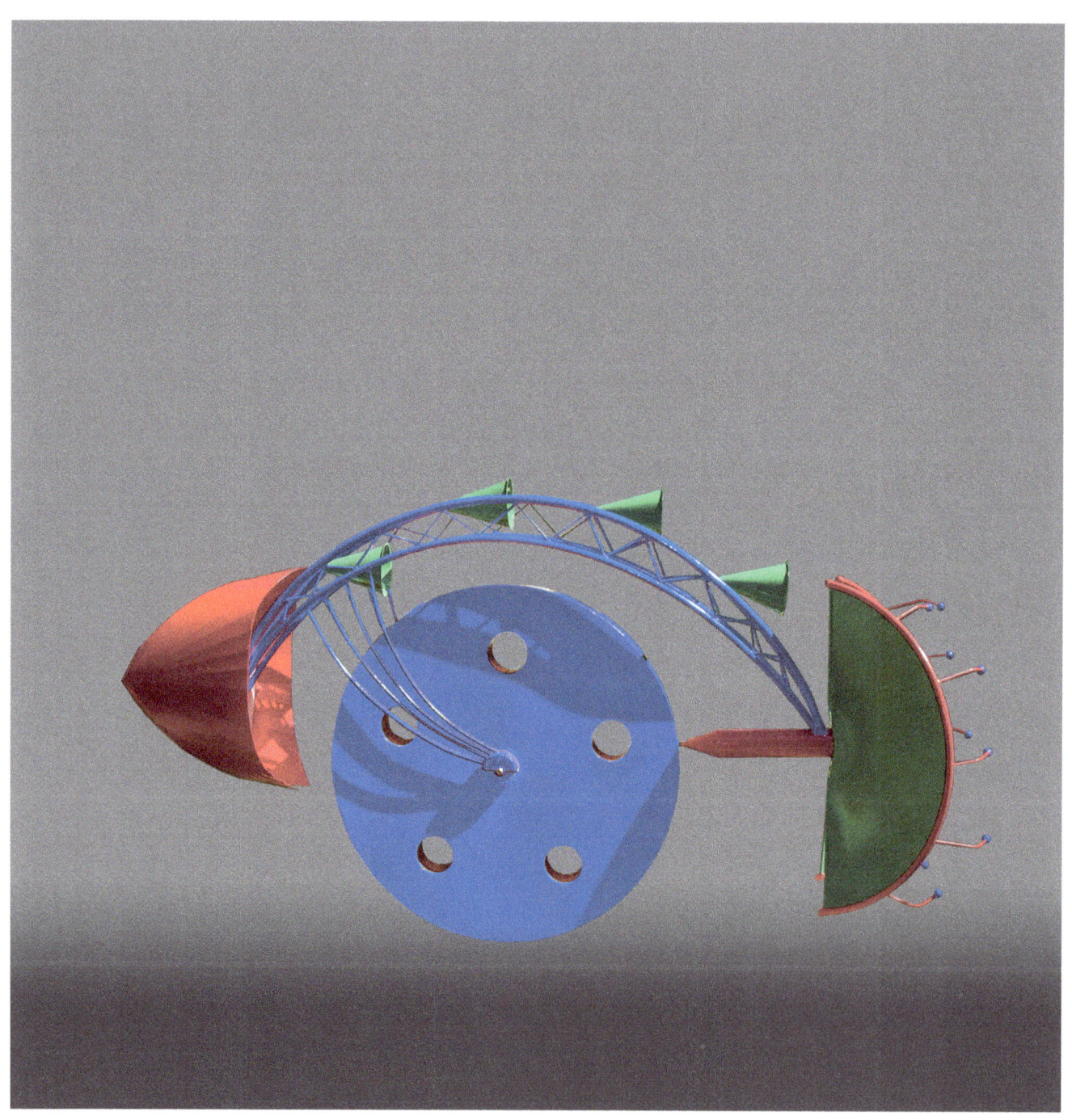

Stan Huncilman, *Hydromaticus*, 2012, Painted steel, 5H x 12L x 3W ft.

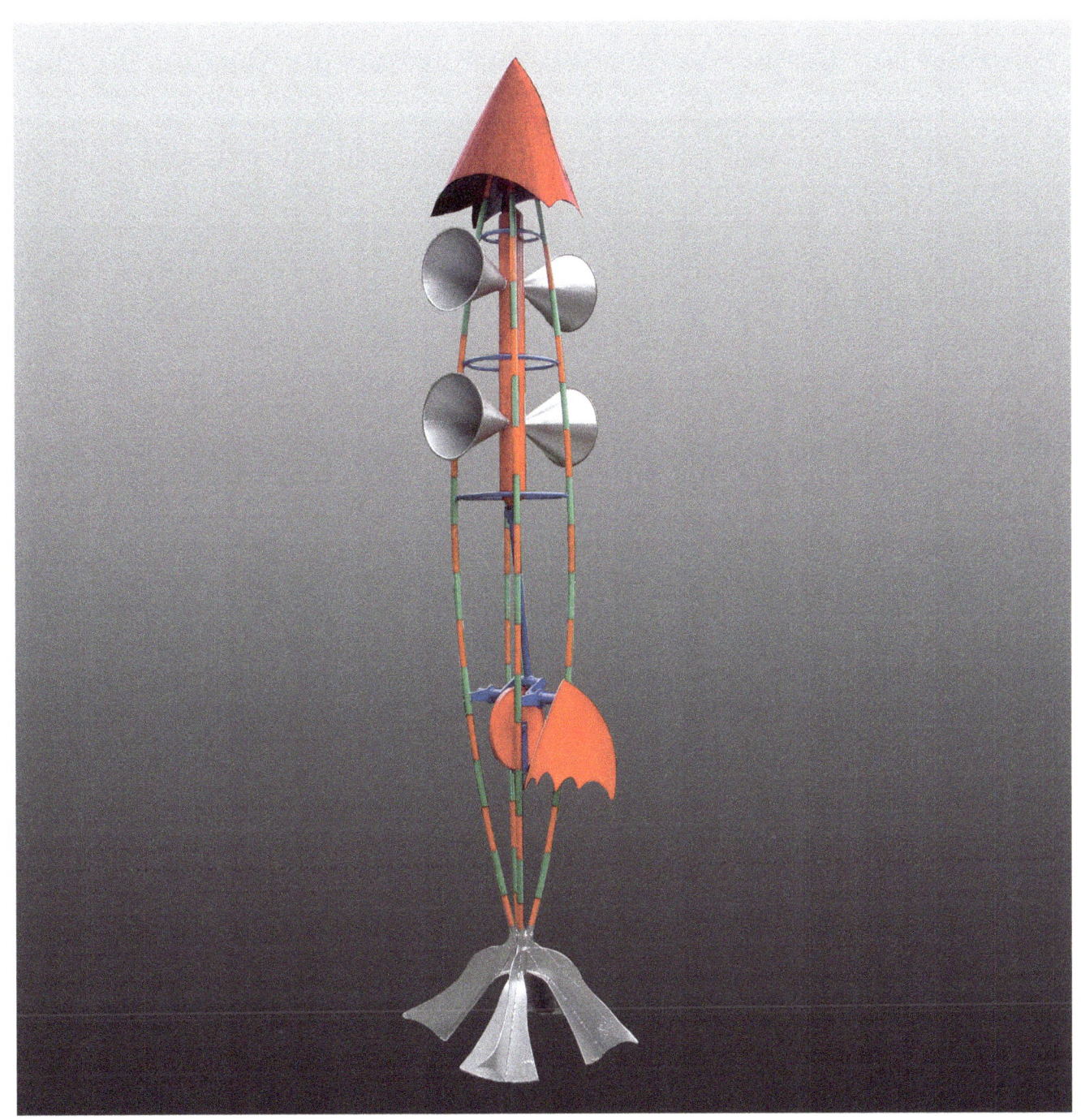

Stan Huncilman, *Tempeste Gotto*, 2011, Painted steel, 12H in. x 3W ft .x 3D ft.

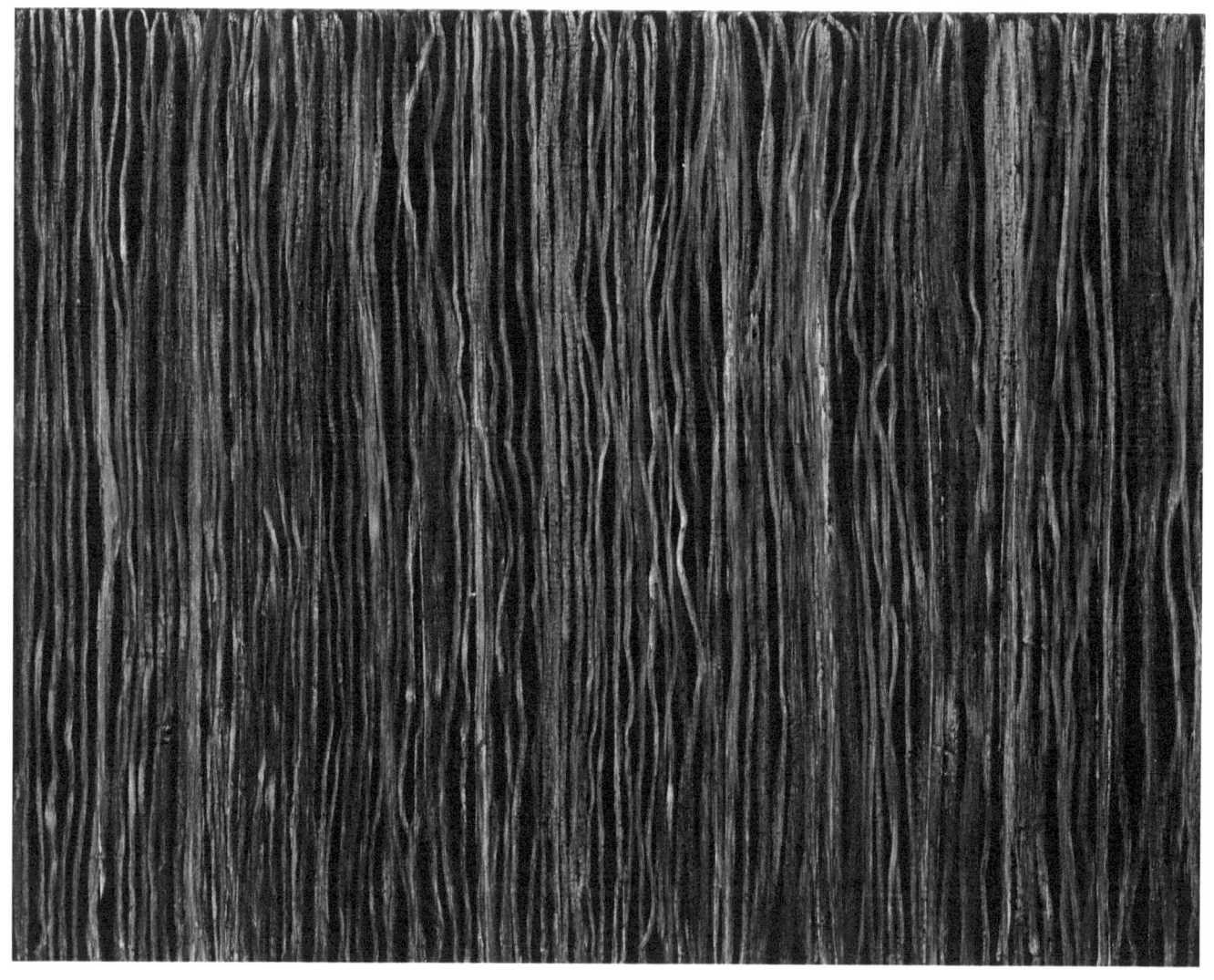

Carol Ladewig, *Doing it Again*, 2012, Oil stick, oil, alkyd on wood panel, 41 x 52.5 in.

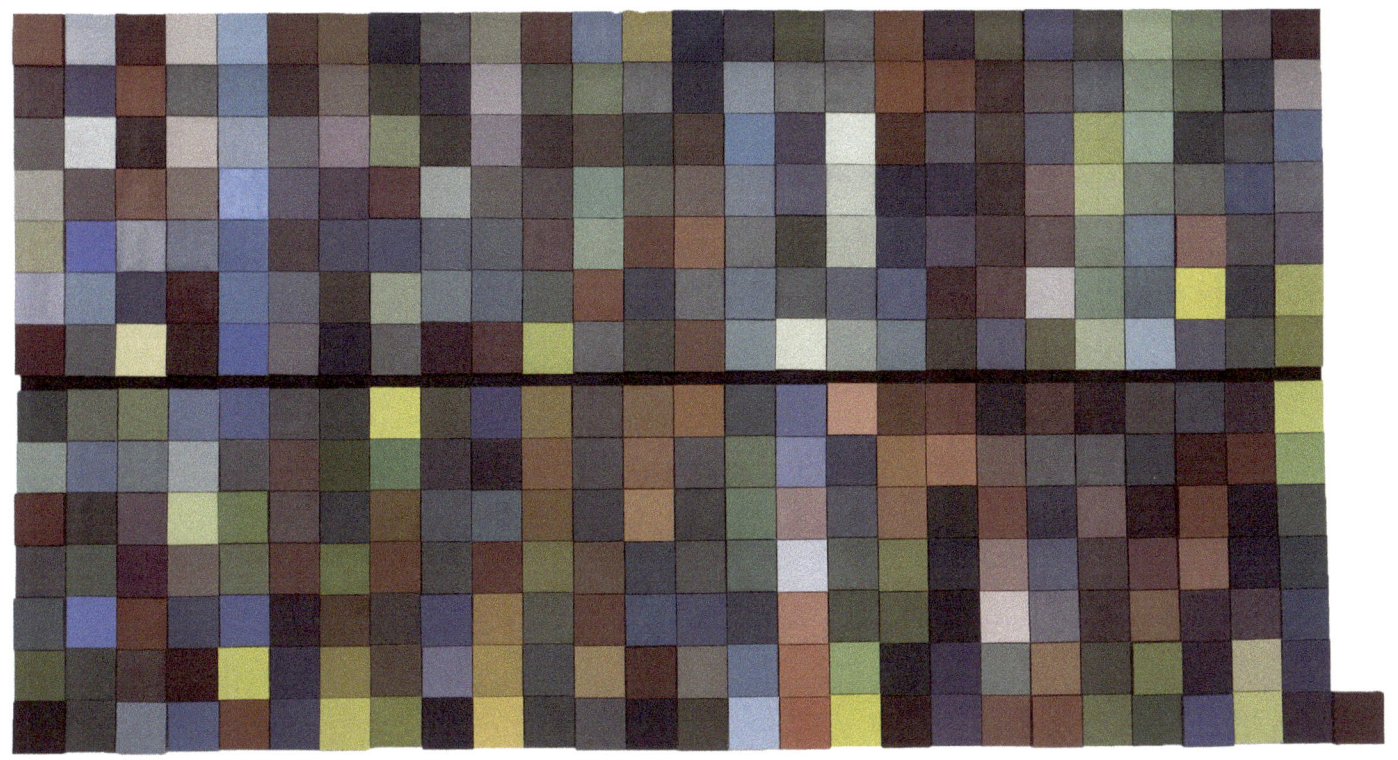

Carol Ladewig, *Year in Color 2011 (5222 weeks + a day)*, 2011, Acrylic and gouache on 365 canvas panels, each panel is 6 x 6 in., and varying depth of 3/4 in, to 1 1/2 in. overall 88 x 162 in. The days hang in units of 7 days.

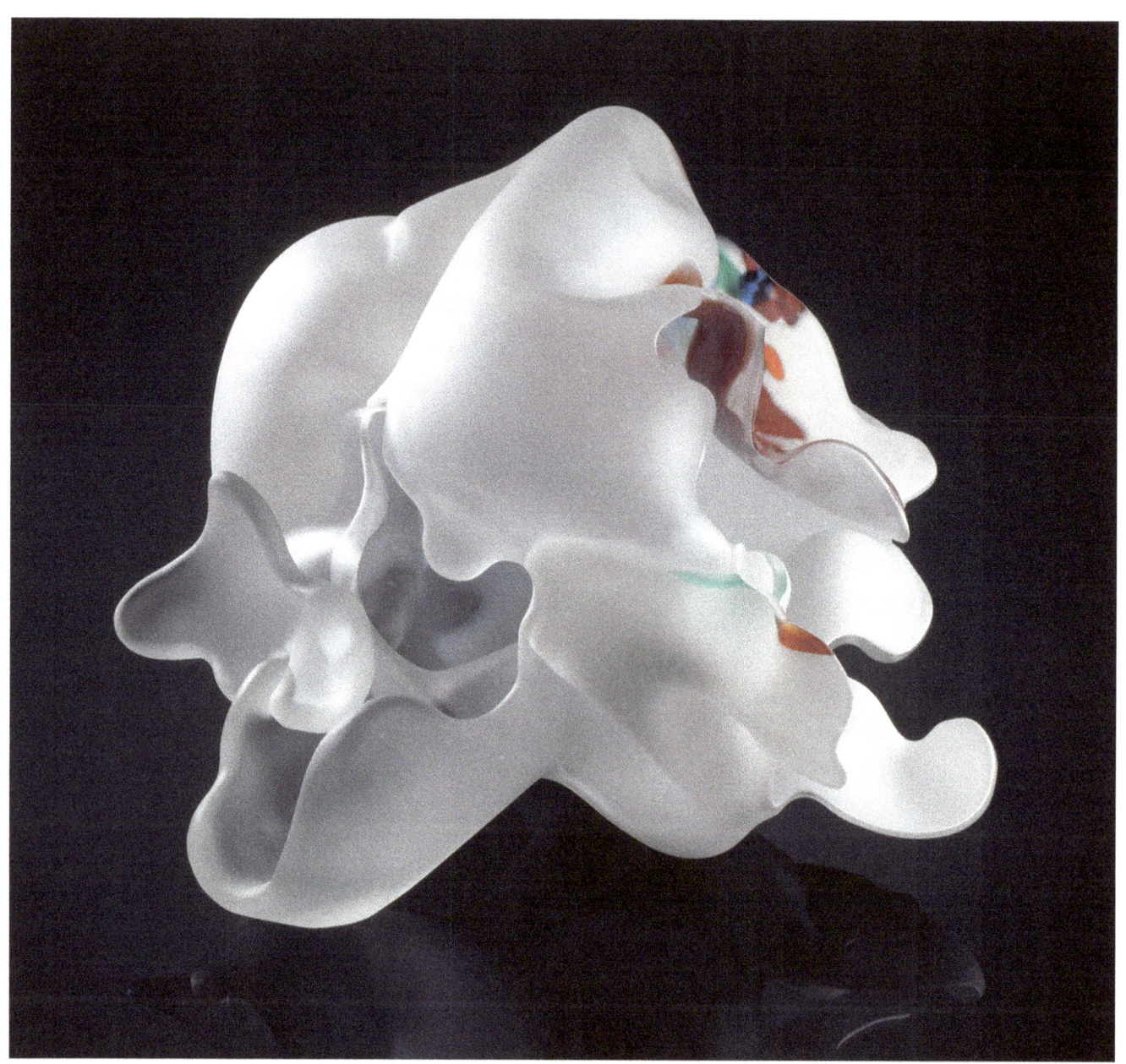

Marvin Lipofsky, *IGS lll #1*, 1988-93, Mold blown glass, cut, sandblasted and acid etched, 15x20 in. Blown at Crystalex Hantich, Novy Bar, Czechoslovakia with help from Stefan Stefko and team, Finished by the artist in his studio. Collection of The Metropolitan Museum of Art, New York. Photo credit: M. Lee Fatherree

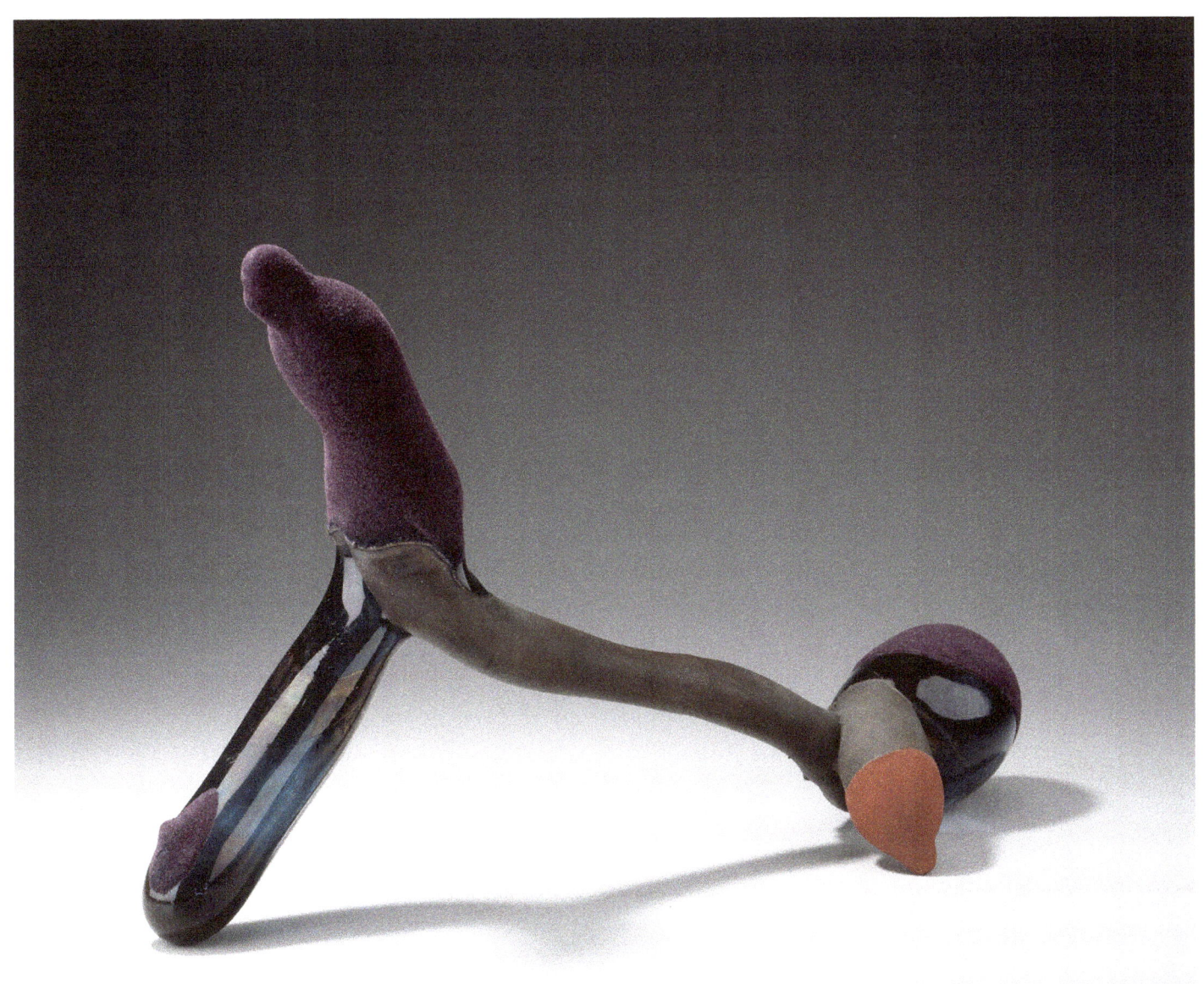

Marvin Lipofsky, *California Loop Series # 38*, 1968, Blown glass, fumed, sandblasted, floatation foam, copper plating, epoxy, and rayon flocking, 14 1/2 x 27 1/2 x 7 1/2 in. Blown at University of California Berkeley. Finished by the artist in the studio, Collection of the Cantor Center for the Arts, Stanford University. Photo: M. Lee Fatherree

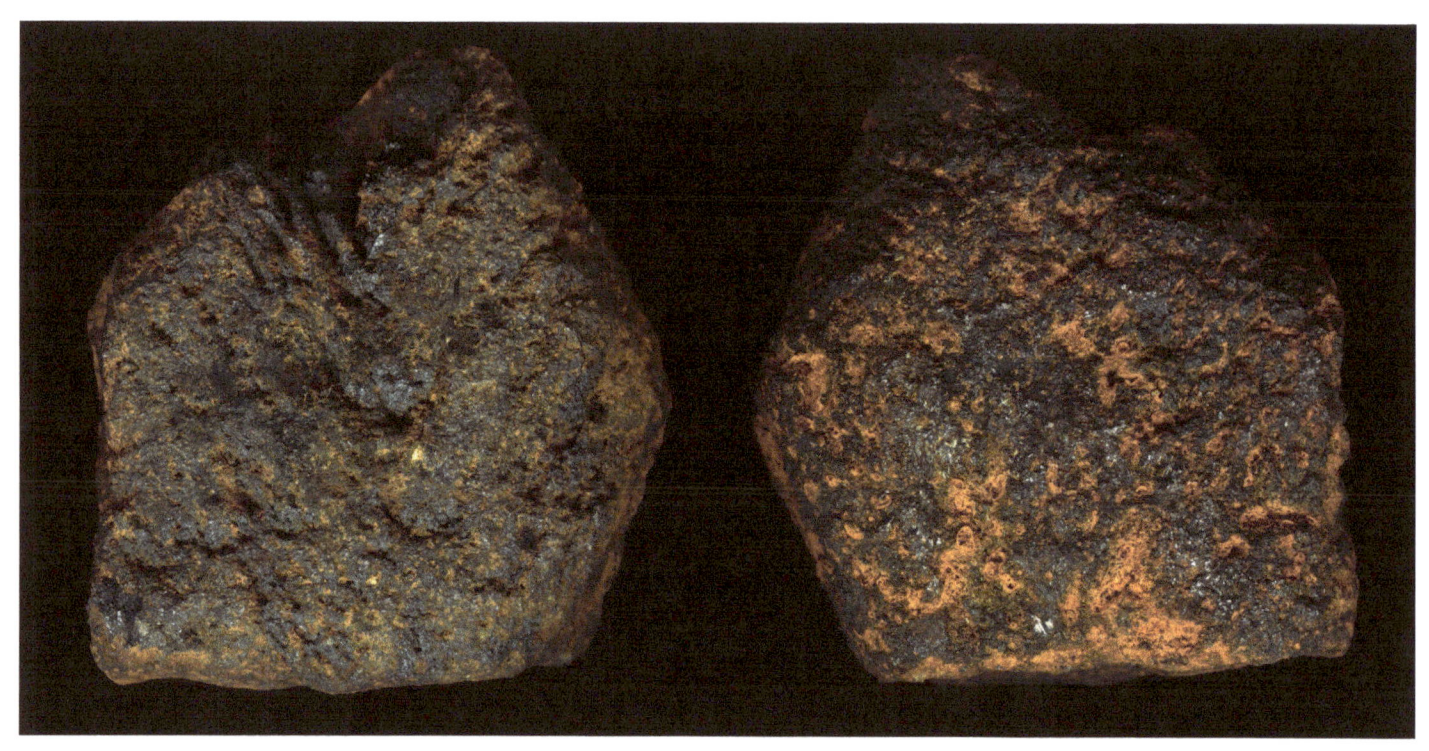

P.G. Meier, *Iron Rocks*, 2012, Archival pigment inkjet on paper, 32 x 16 in.

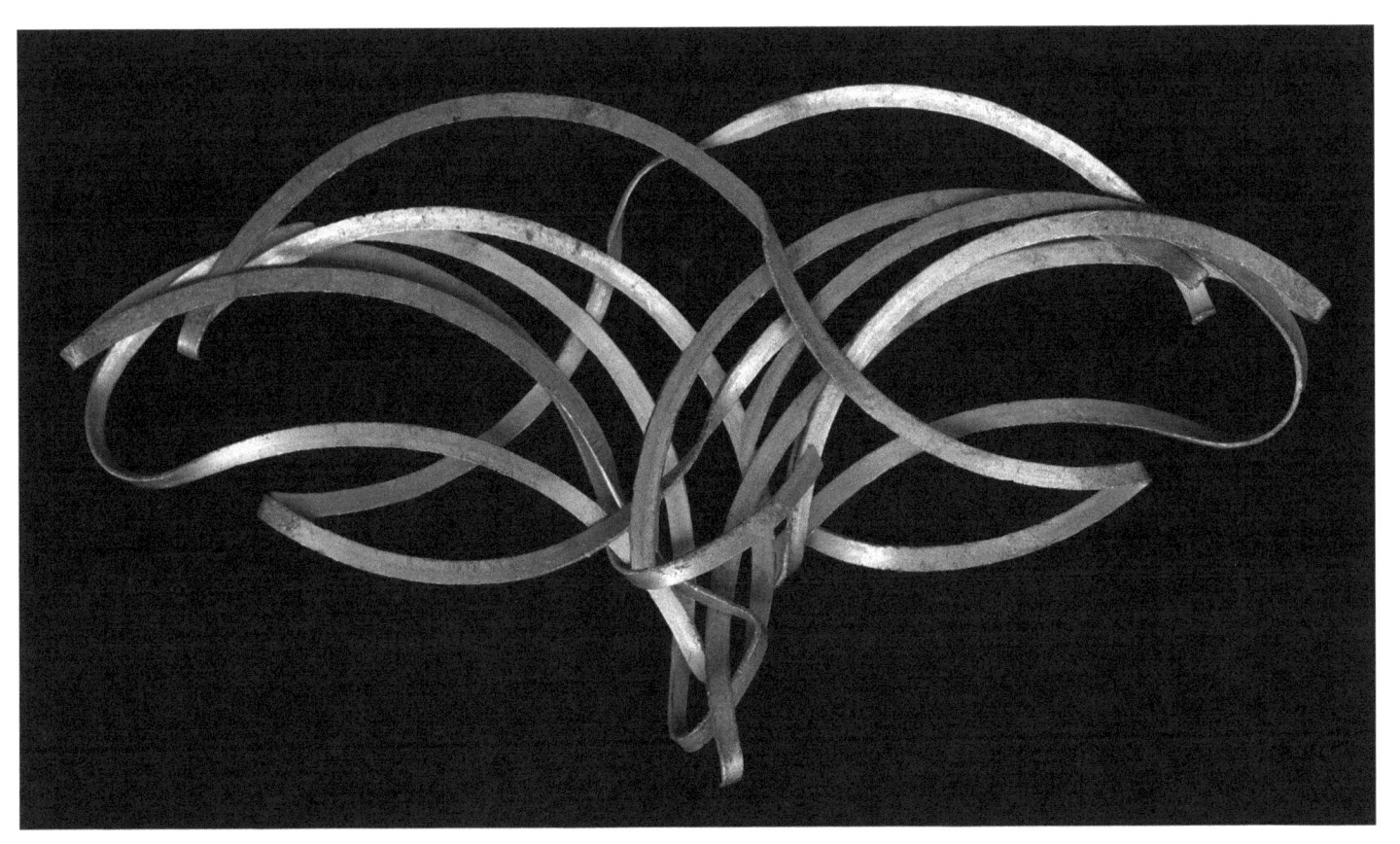

P.G. Meier, *Combined*, 2010, Archival pigment inkjet on paper, 28 x 16 in.

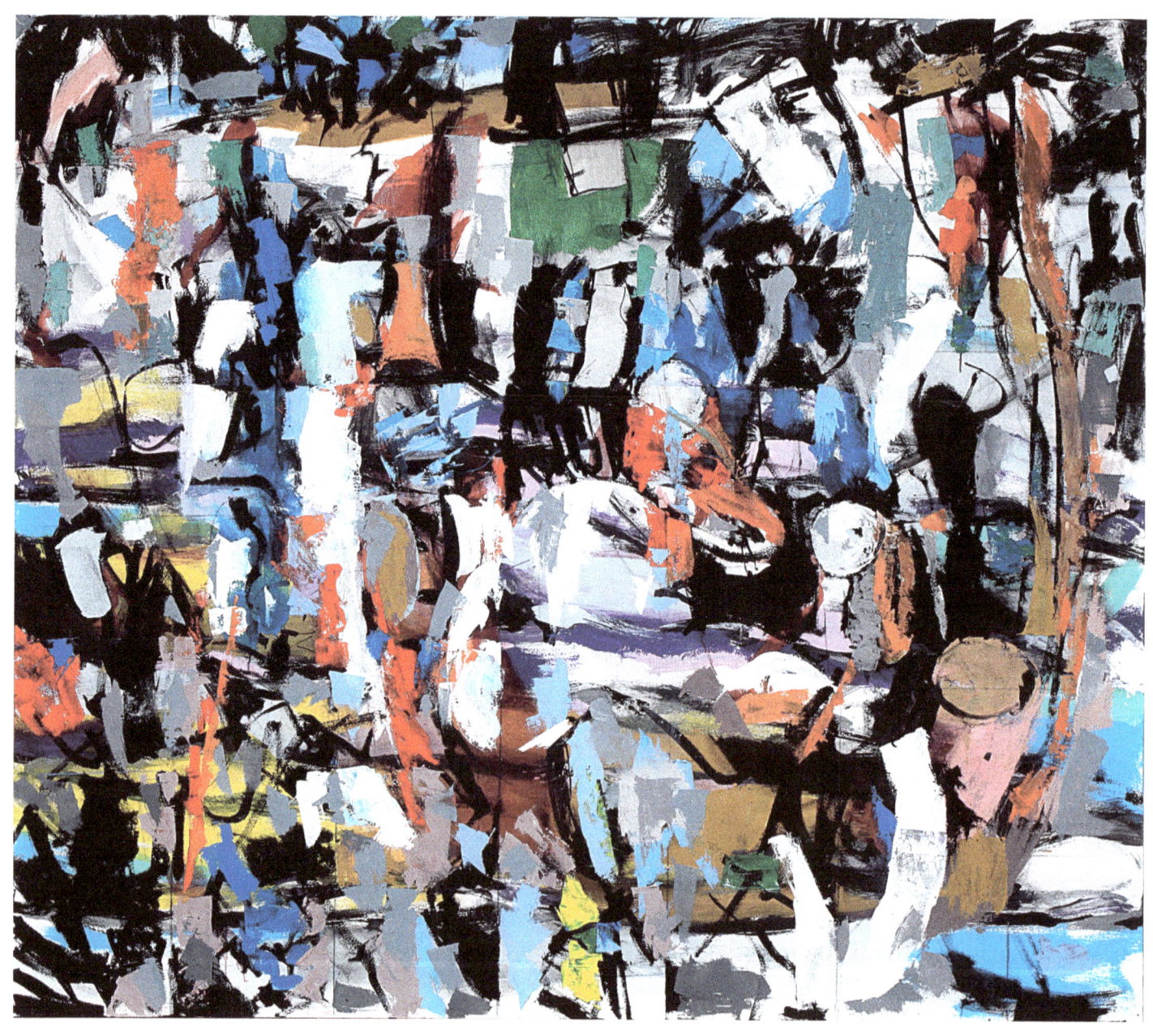

Arthur Monroe, *Unnamed*, 2011, Oil on canvas, 76 x 84 in.

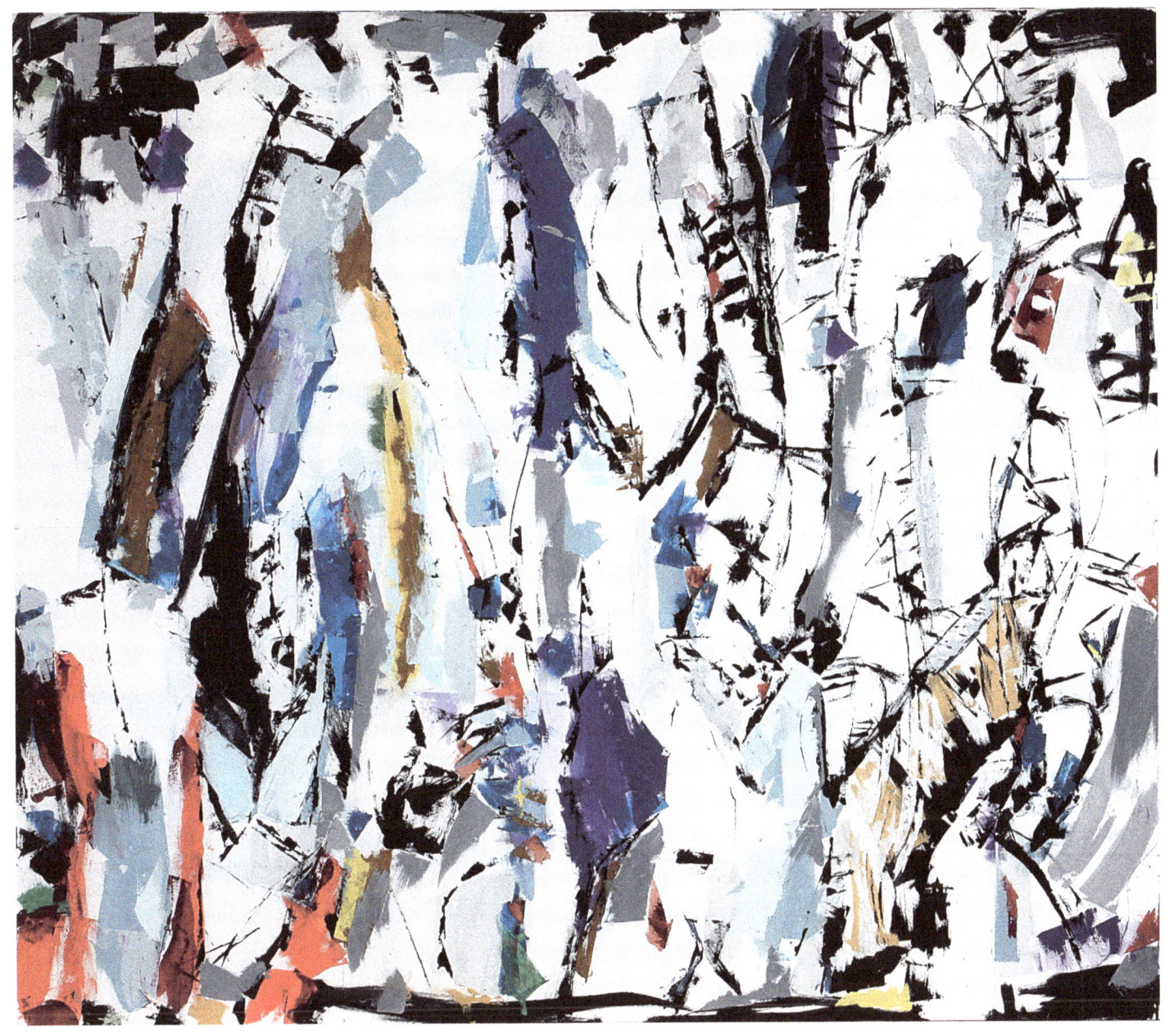

Arthur Monroe, *Unnamed*, 2011, Oil on canvas, 76 x 84 in.

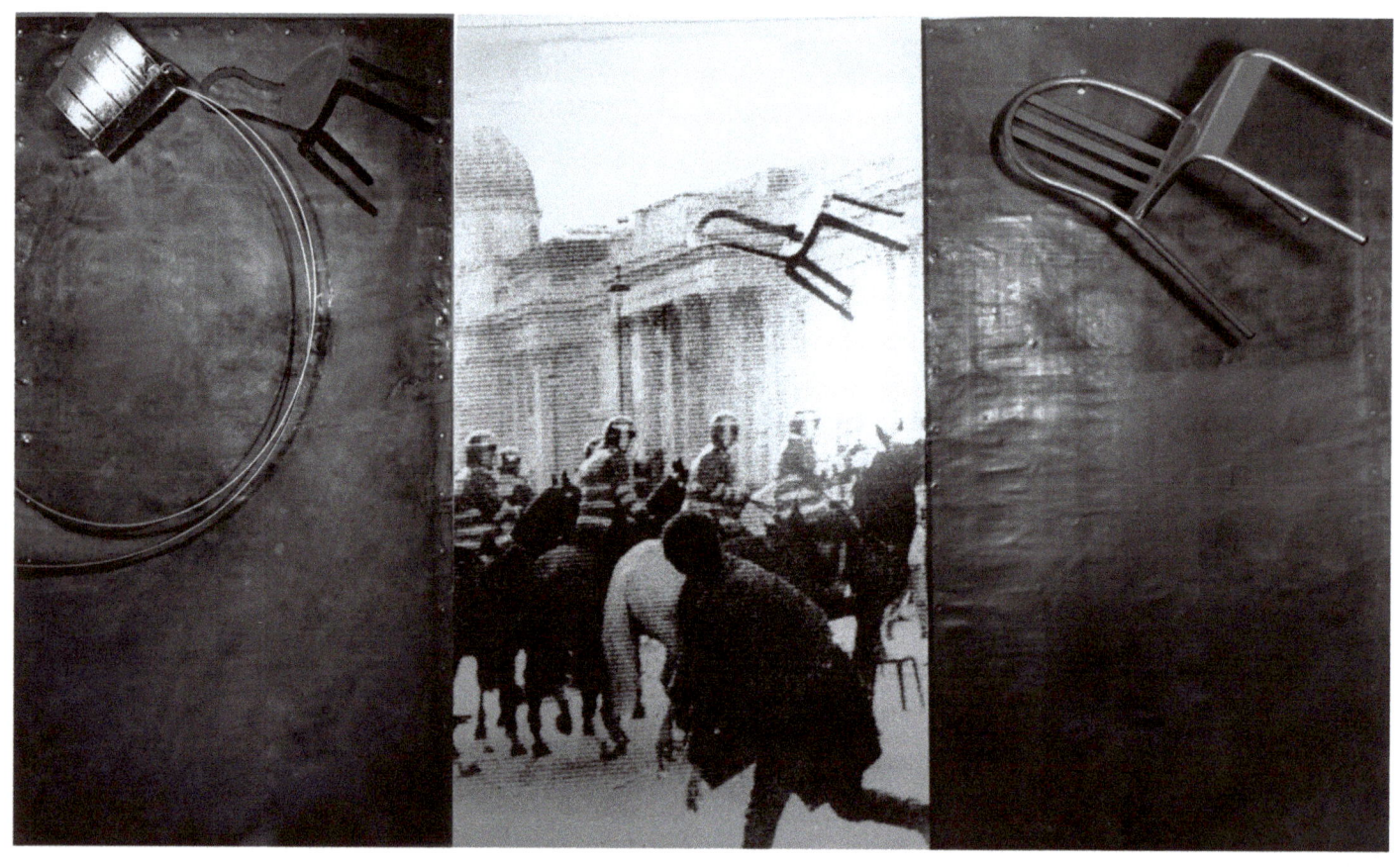

Guillermo Pulido, *Unseating Gravity*, 1997, Chair, photo image on tin and lead, 12 x 8 ft.

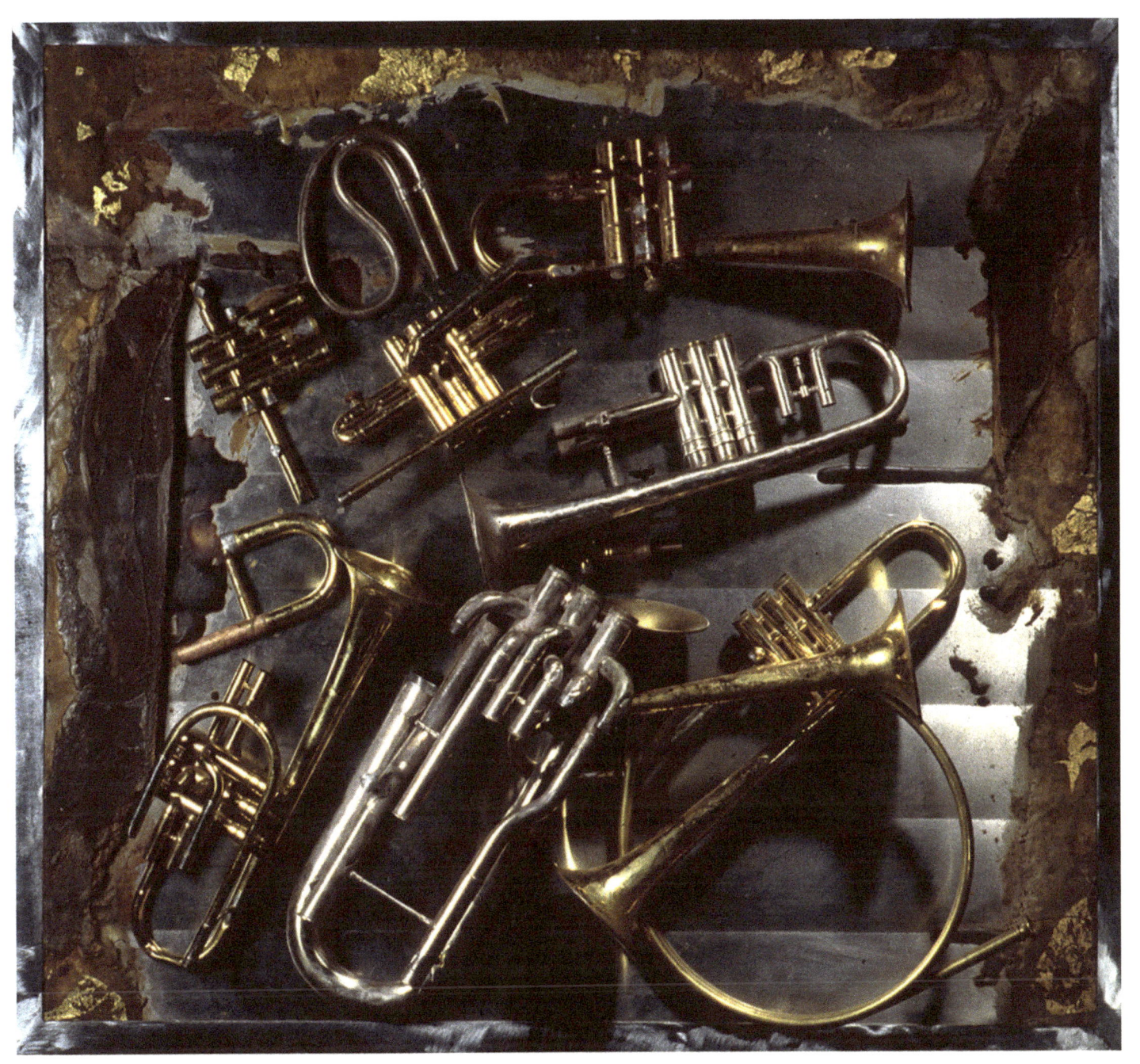

Guillermo Pulido, *Dissonance*, 2001, Wax, brass on aluminum, 36 x 40 in.

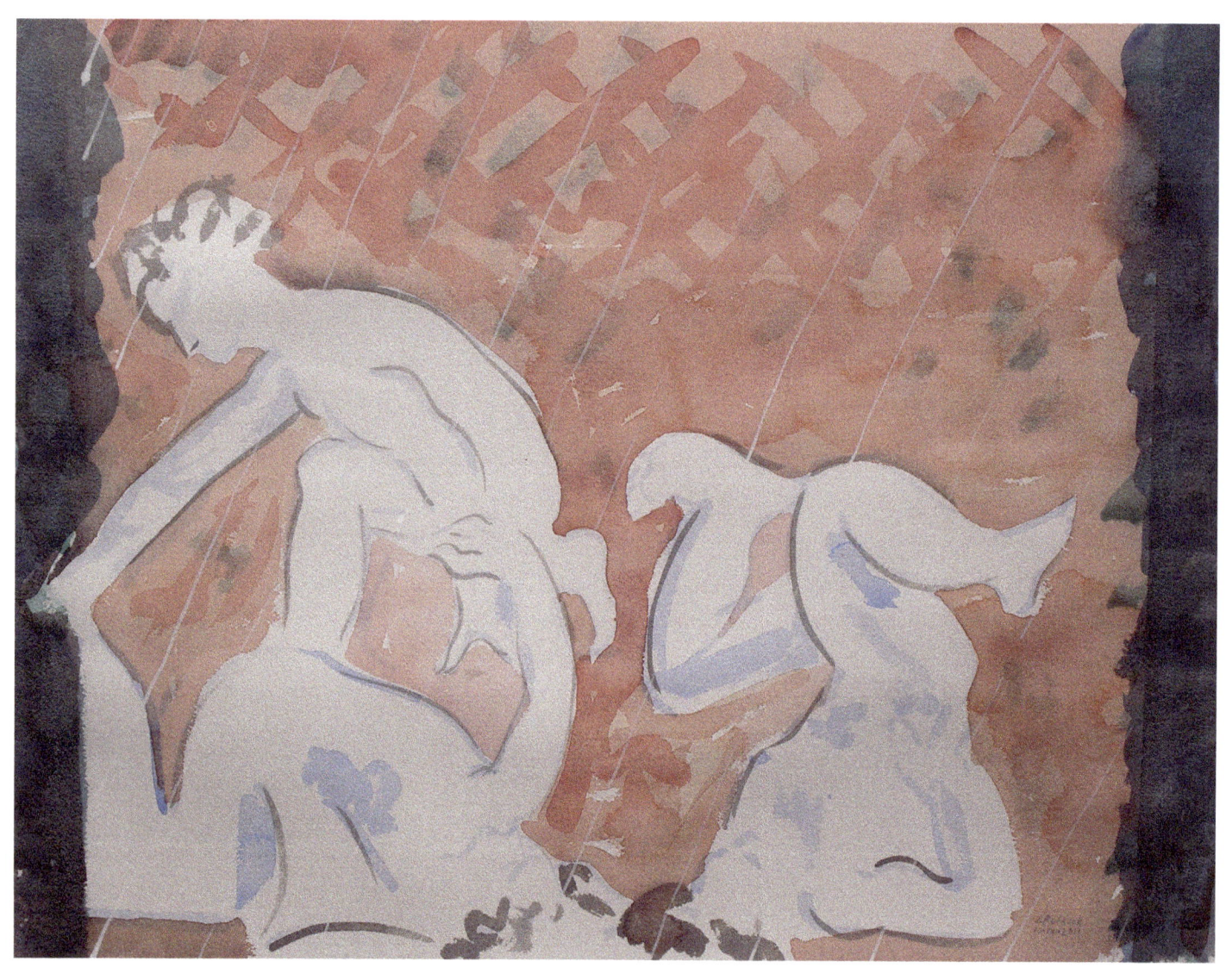

Loren Rehbock, *Break Dancer Study 2*, 2011, Watercolor, 18 x 24 in.

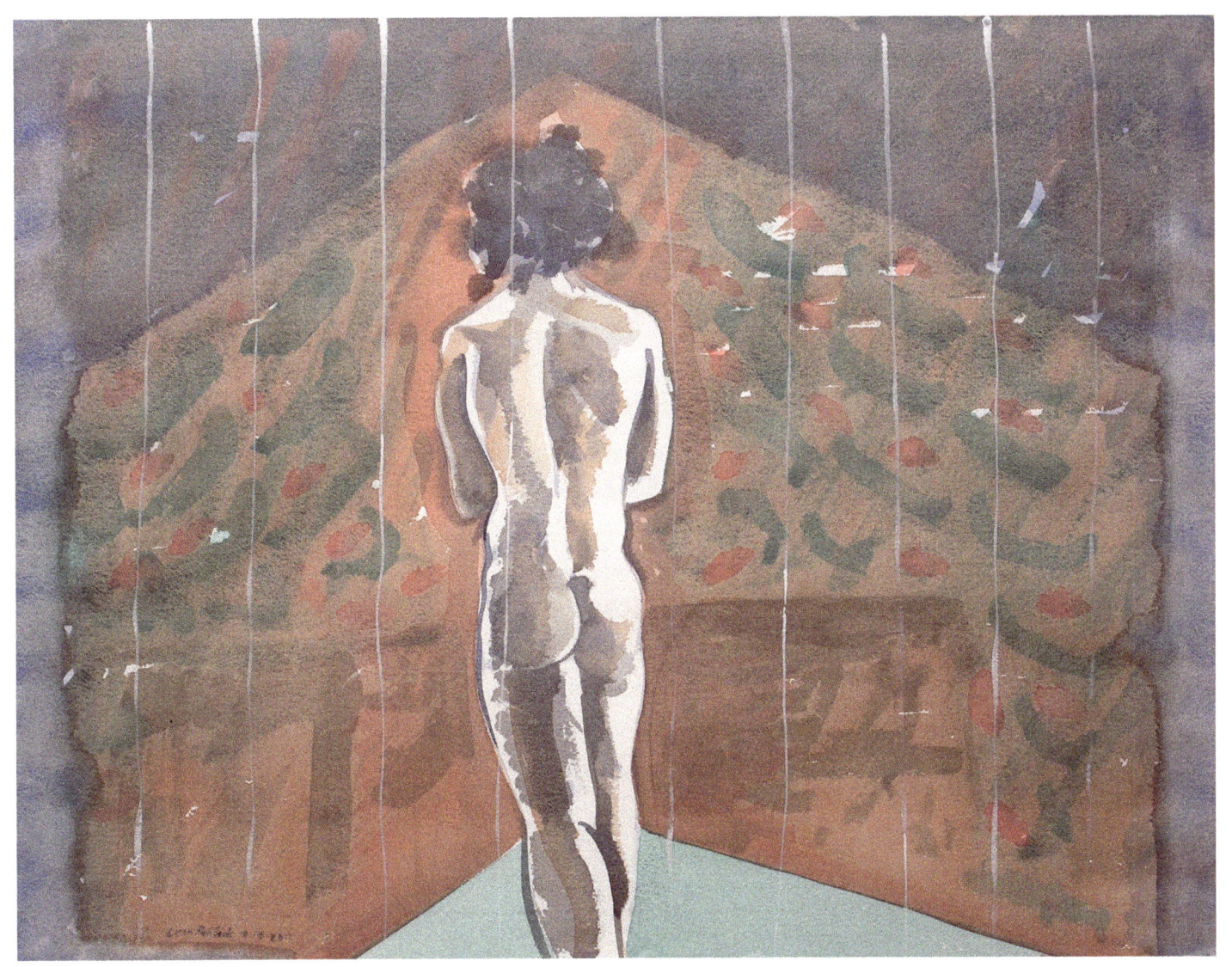

Loren Rehbock, *Break Dancer Study 1*, 2011, Watercolor, 18 x 24 in.

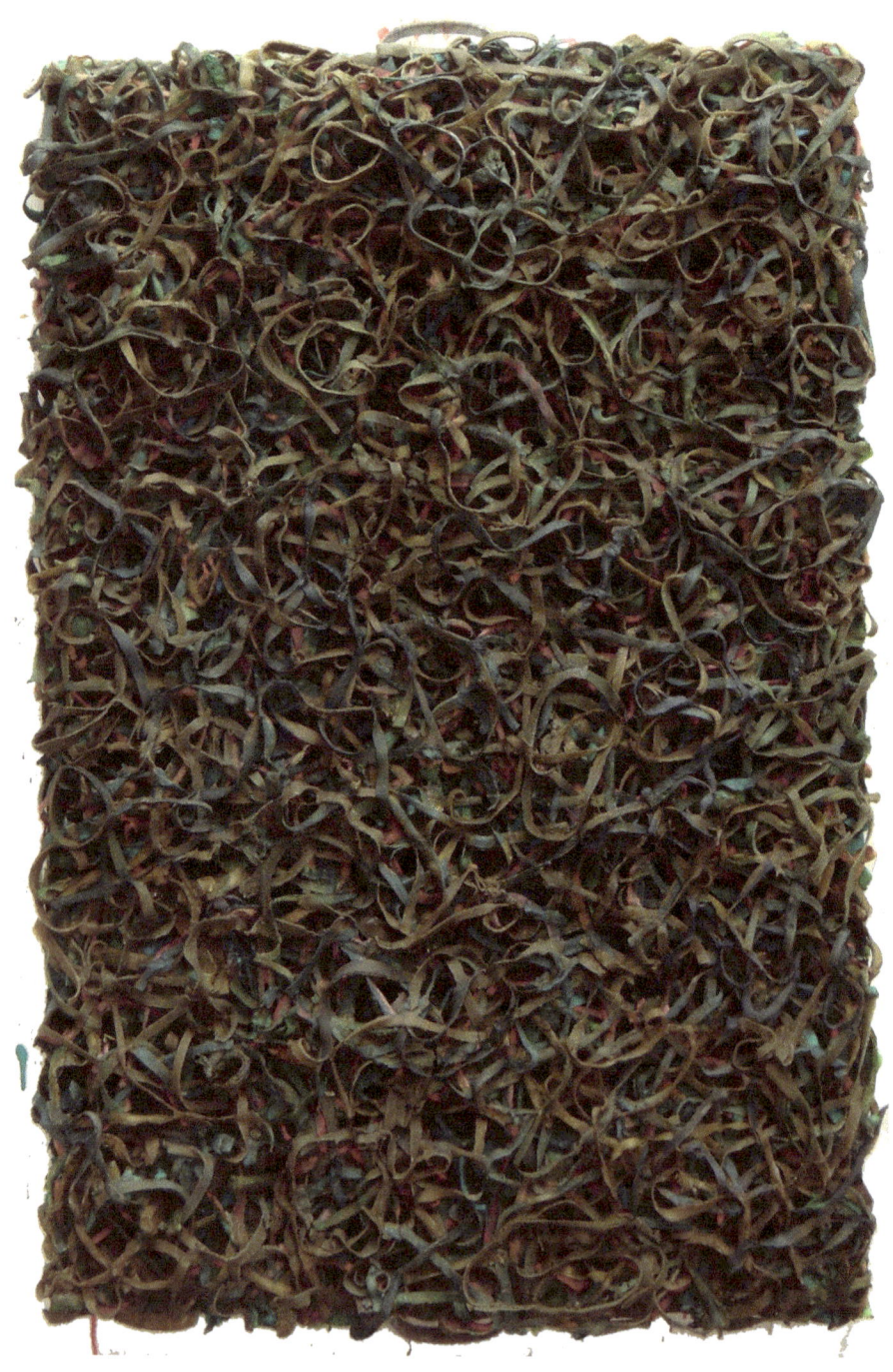

Bill Rosen, *Untitled #12*, 2011, Oil, wax, resins on canvas over 1/8 in. plywood, 37 x 27 x 3 in.

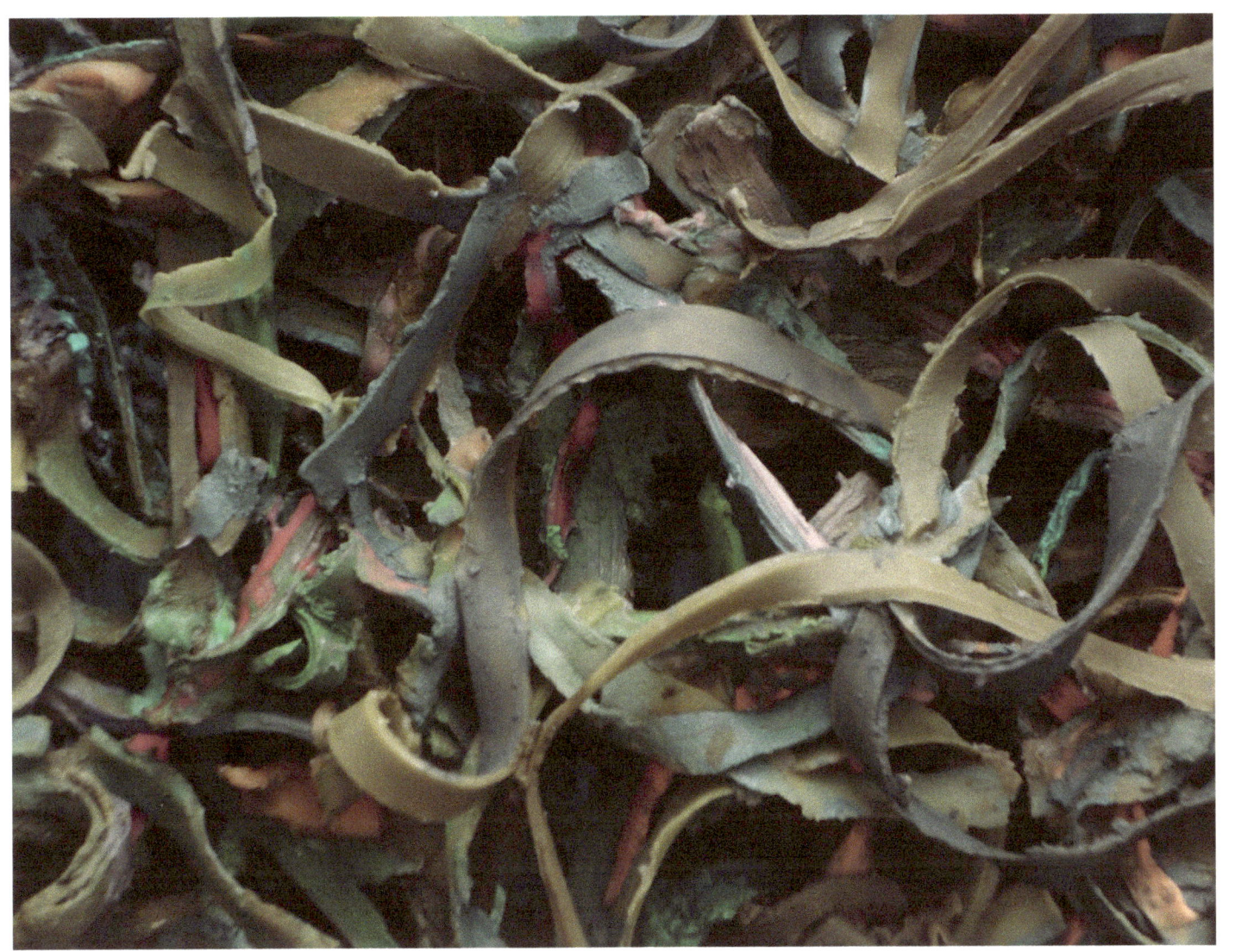

Bill Rosen, *Detail (Untitled #12)*, 8 x 8 x 3 in.

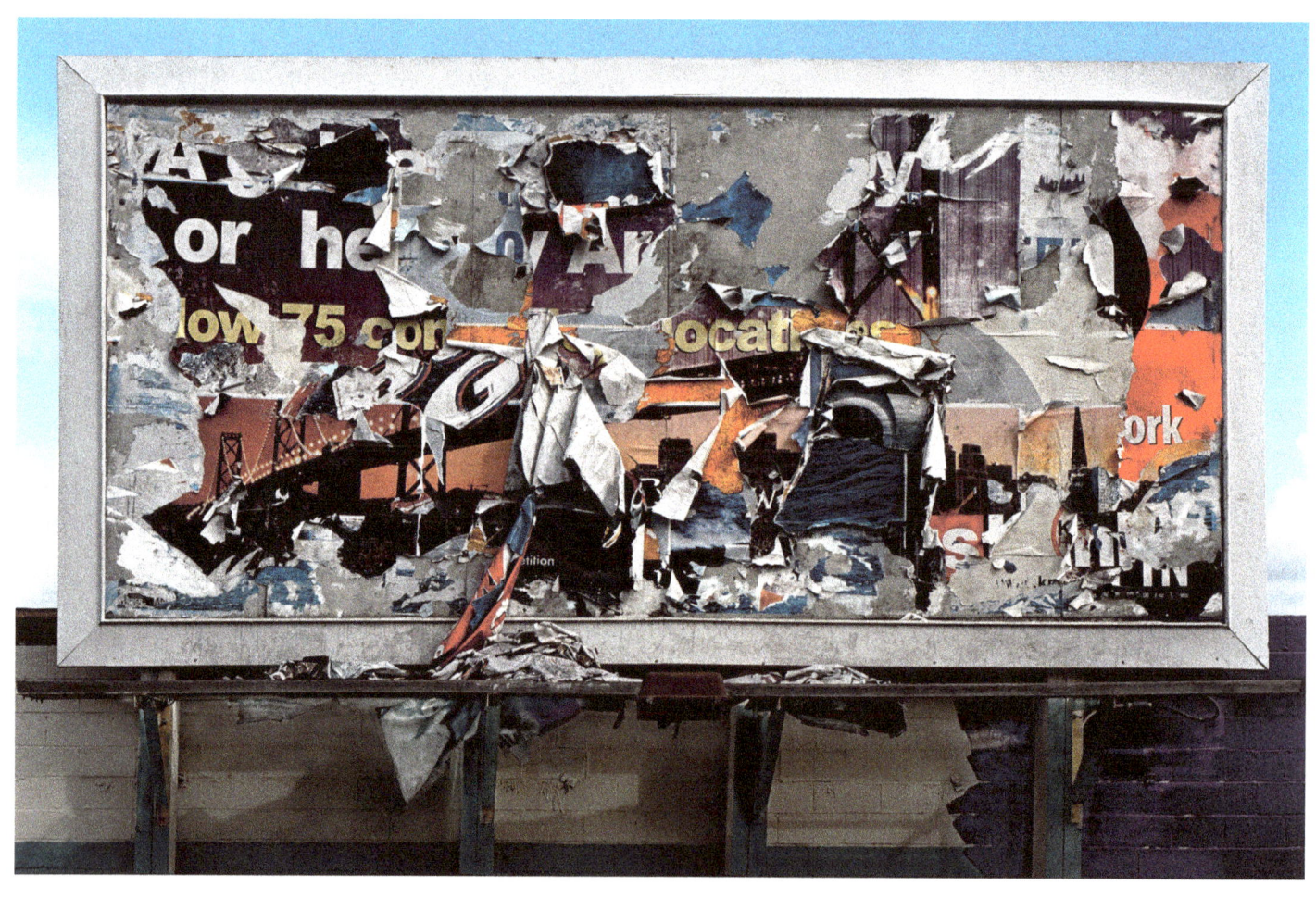

Richard Sargent, *Bay Bridge, Richmond on Barrett Avenue*, 2011, Photograph

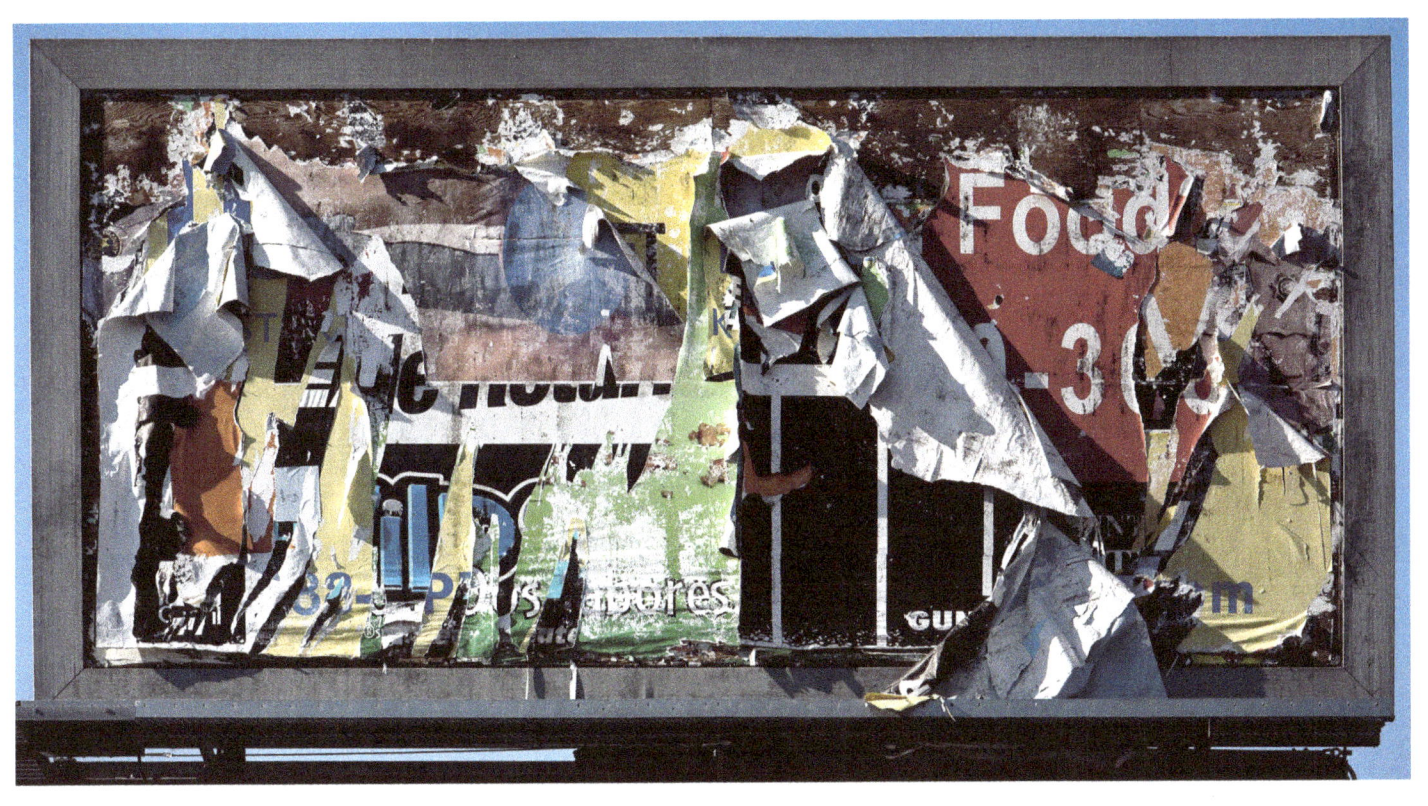

Richard Sargent, *Food Salade*, Oakland at 23rd and East 12th, 2011, Photograph

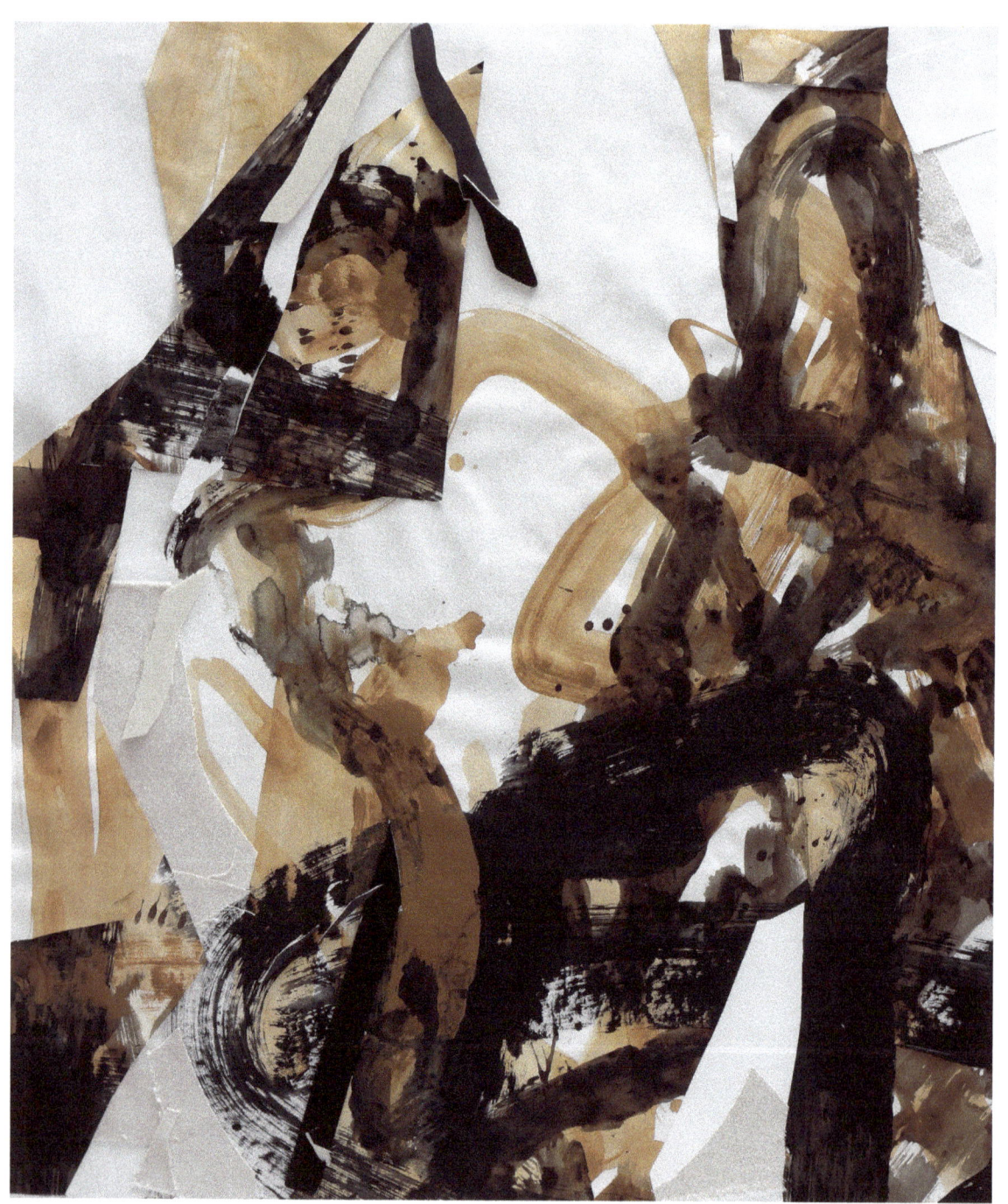

Foad Satterfield, *Tangle Series #13*, 2012, Mixed media, acrylic paint, ink, paper and wood, 44 x 40 in.

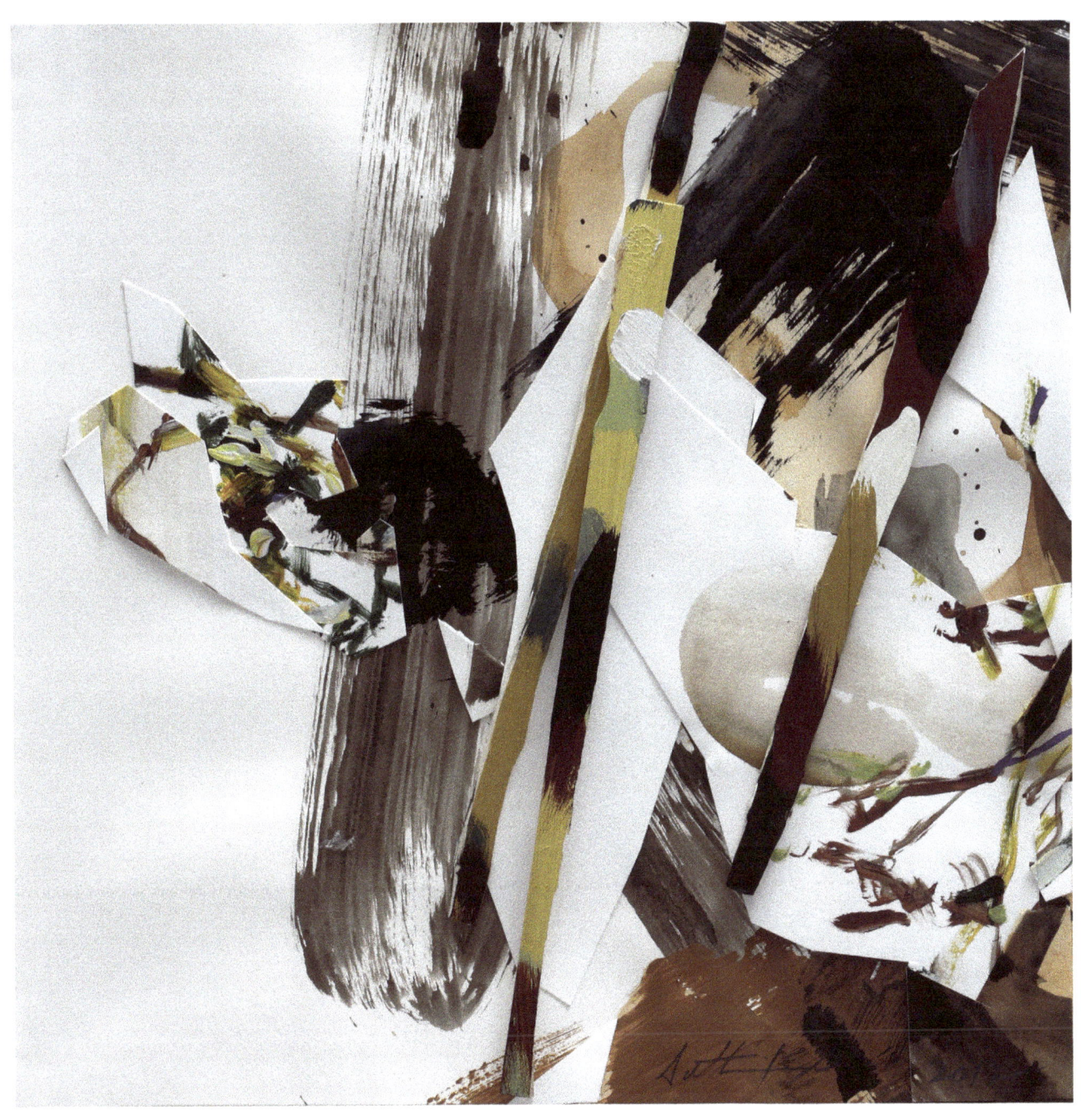

Foad Satterfield, *Tangle Series #5*, 2012, Mixed media, acrylic paint, ink, paper, canvas and wood, 44 x 40 in.

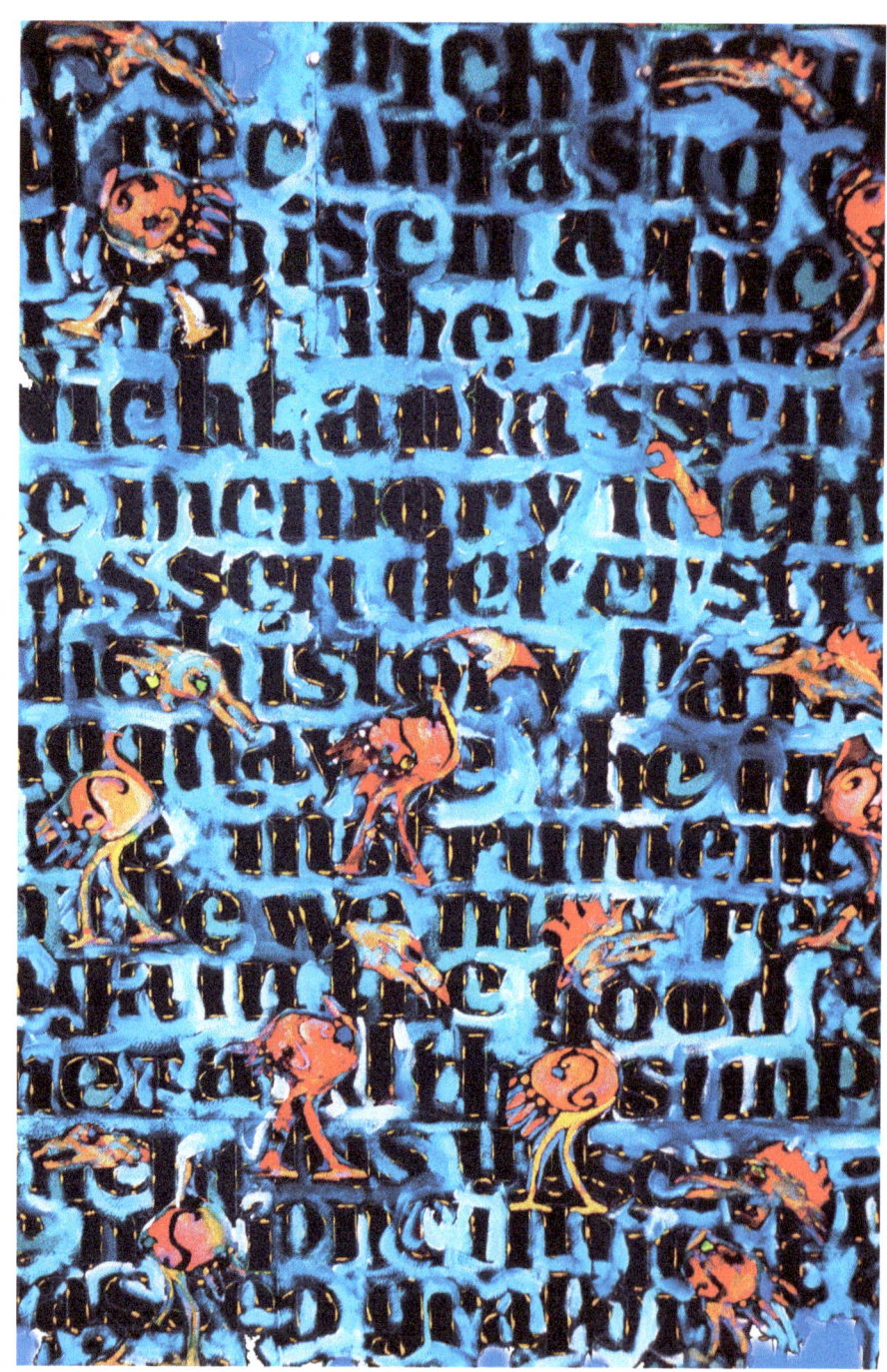

Robert Simons, *Fierze*, 2008, Oil, acrylic and pencil on paper, 44 x 30 in.

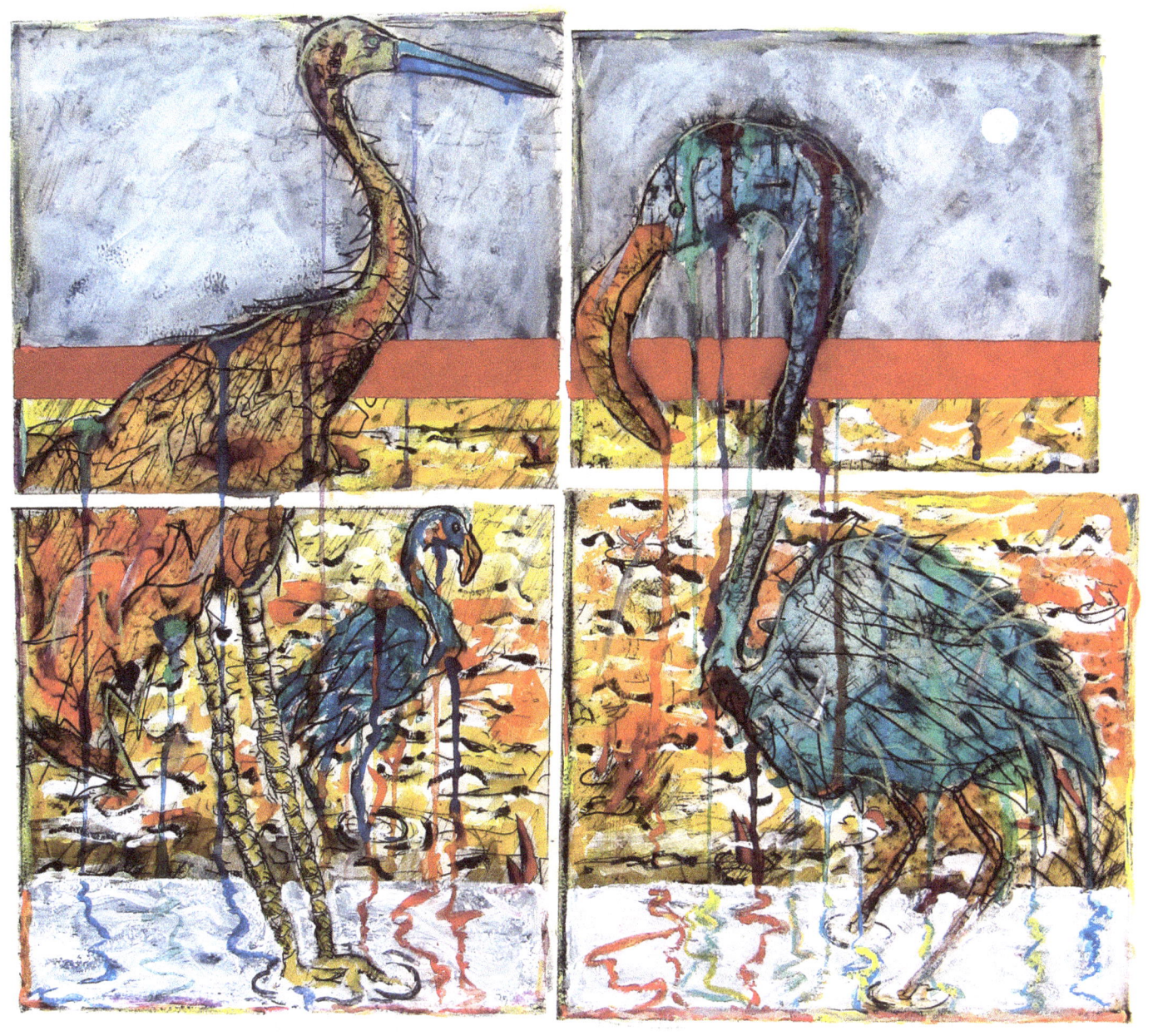

Robert Simons, *Blind Stork and Flamingo Series Number 10*, 2011, Drypoint engraving, gouache, acrylic and ink, 18 x 36 in.

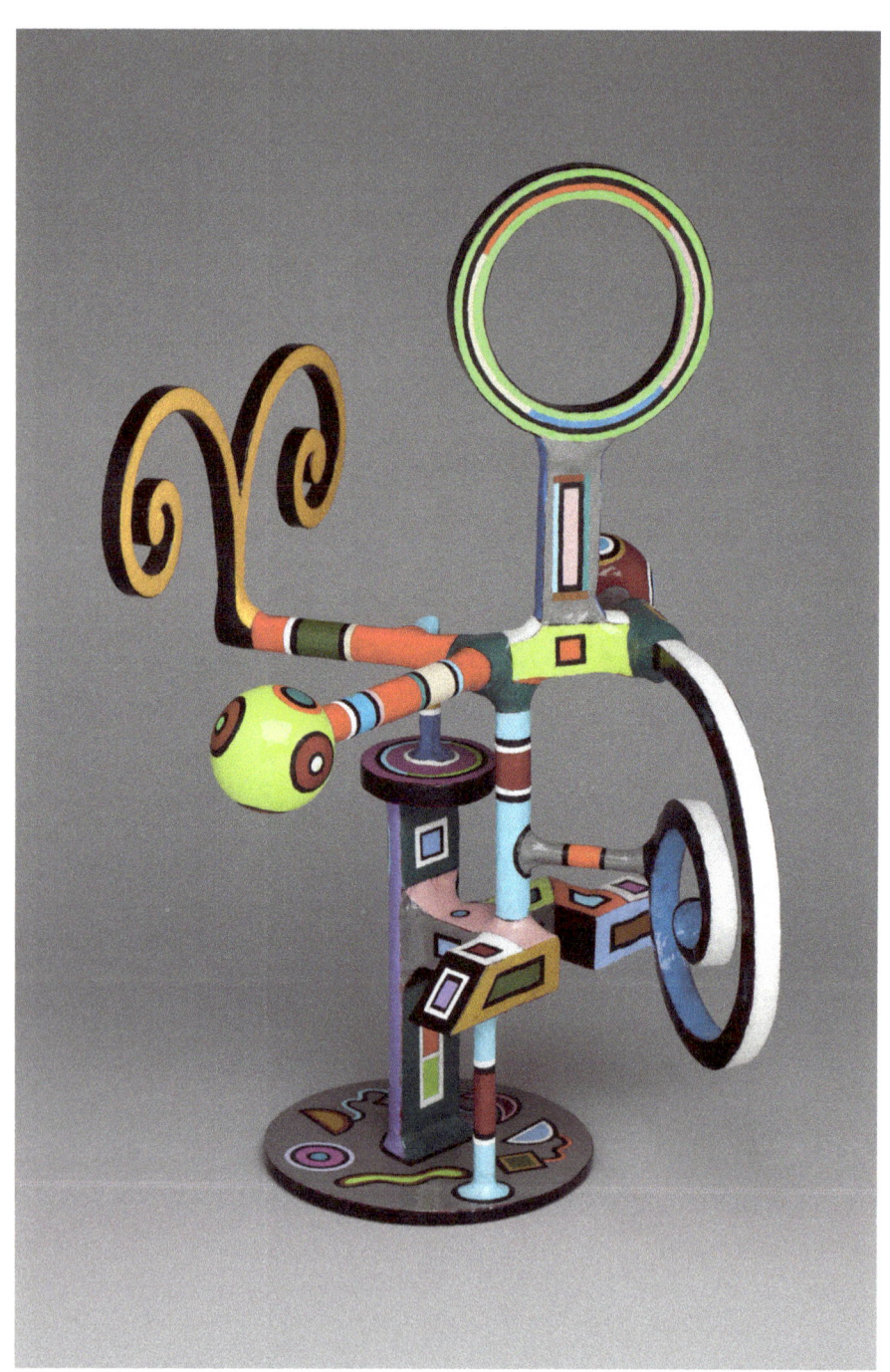

Joseph Slusky, *Wamba*, 2011, Steel and acrylic laquer paint, 17 3/4H x 12L x 11W in.

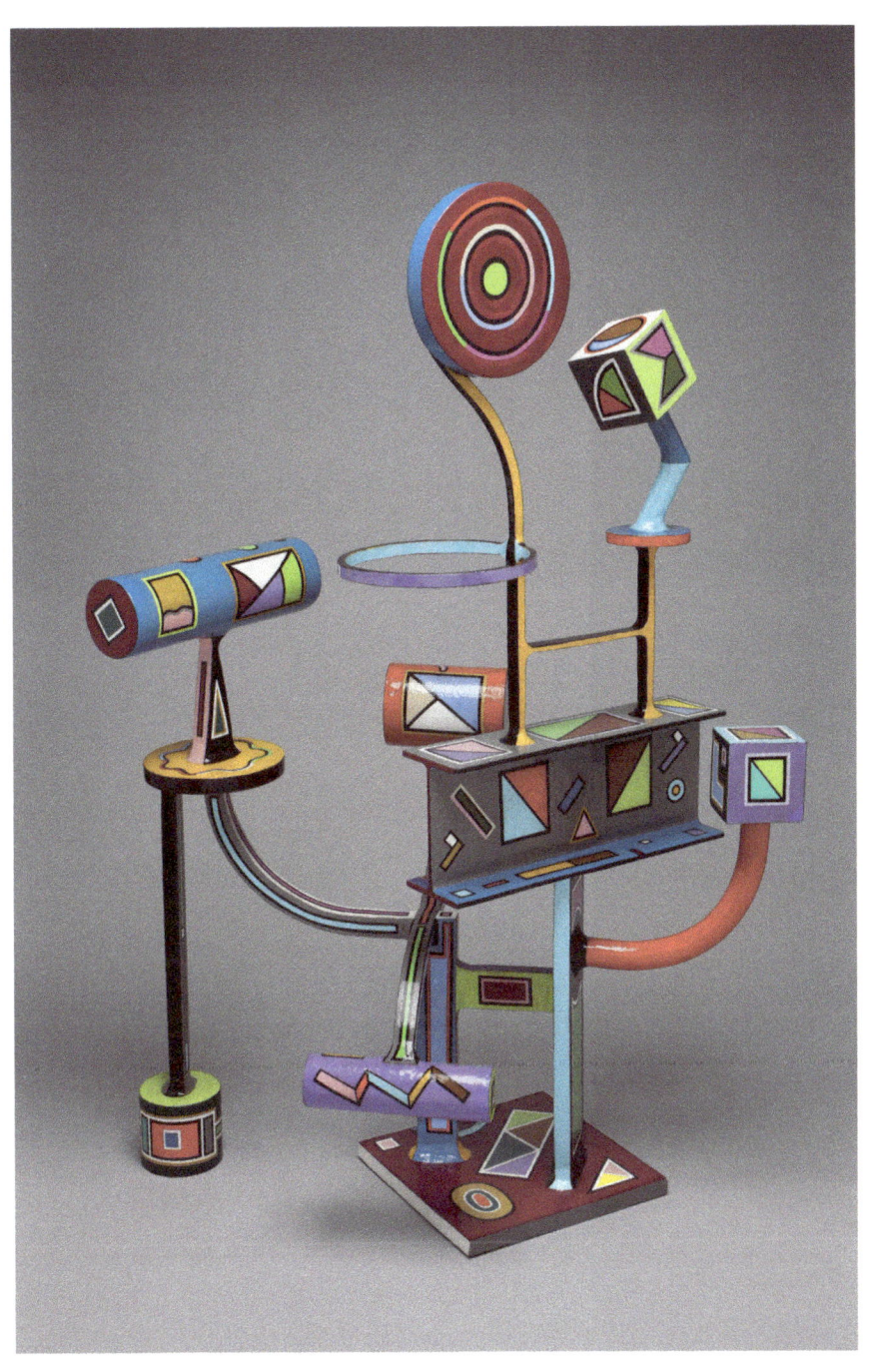

Joseph Slusky, *Helios*, 2002, Steel and acrylic laquer paint, 48H x 36L x 22W in.

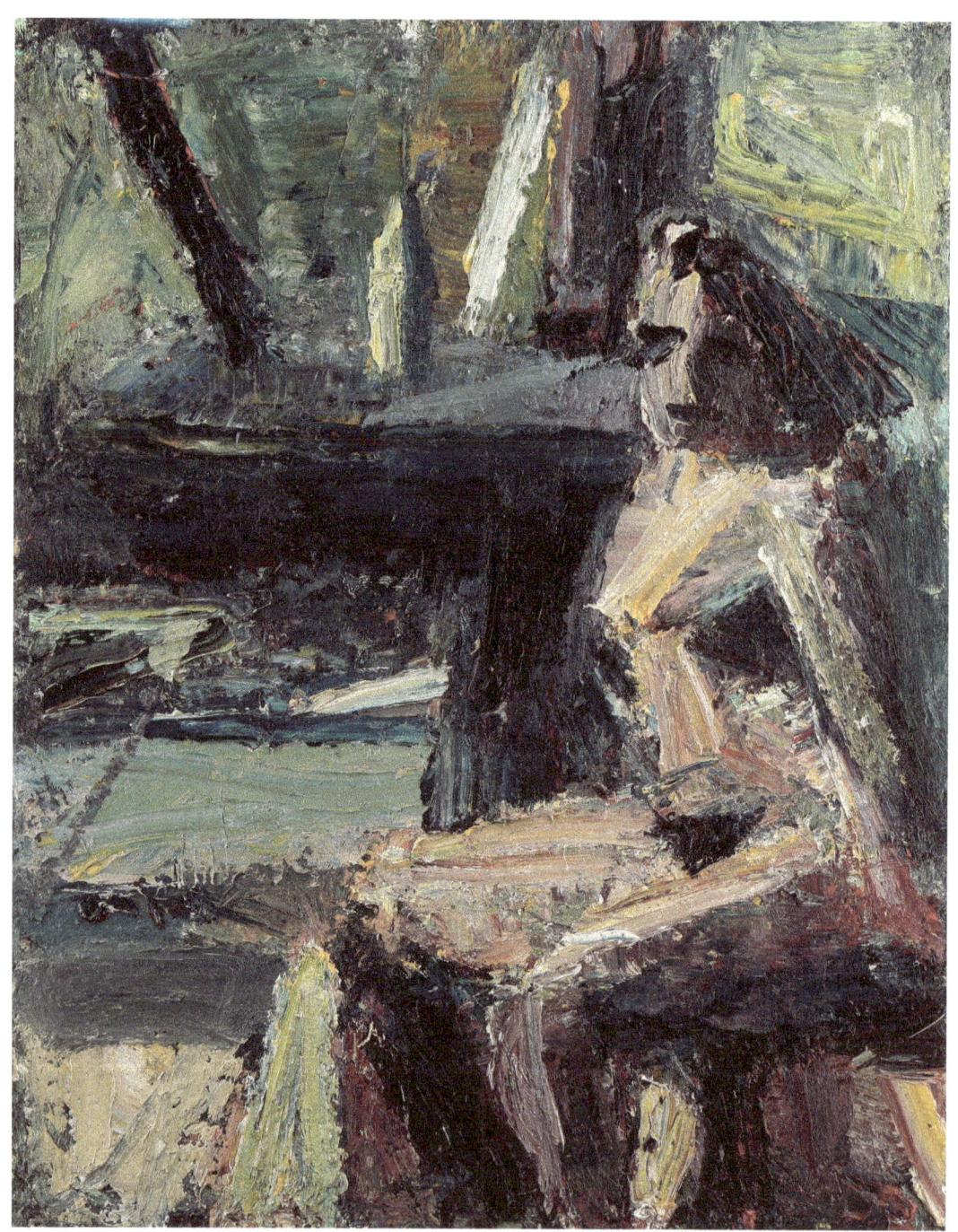

Terry St. John, *Solveig*, 2011, Oil on canvas, 60 x 48 in.

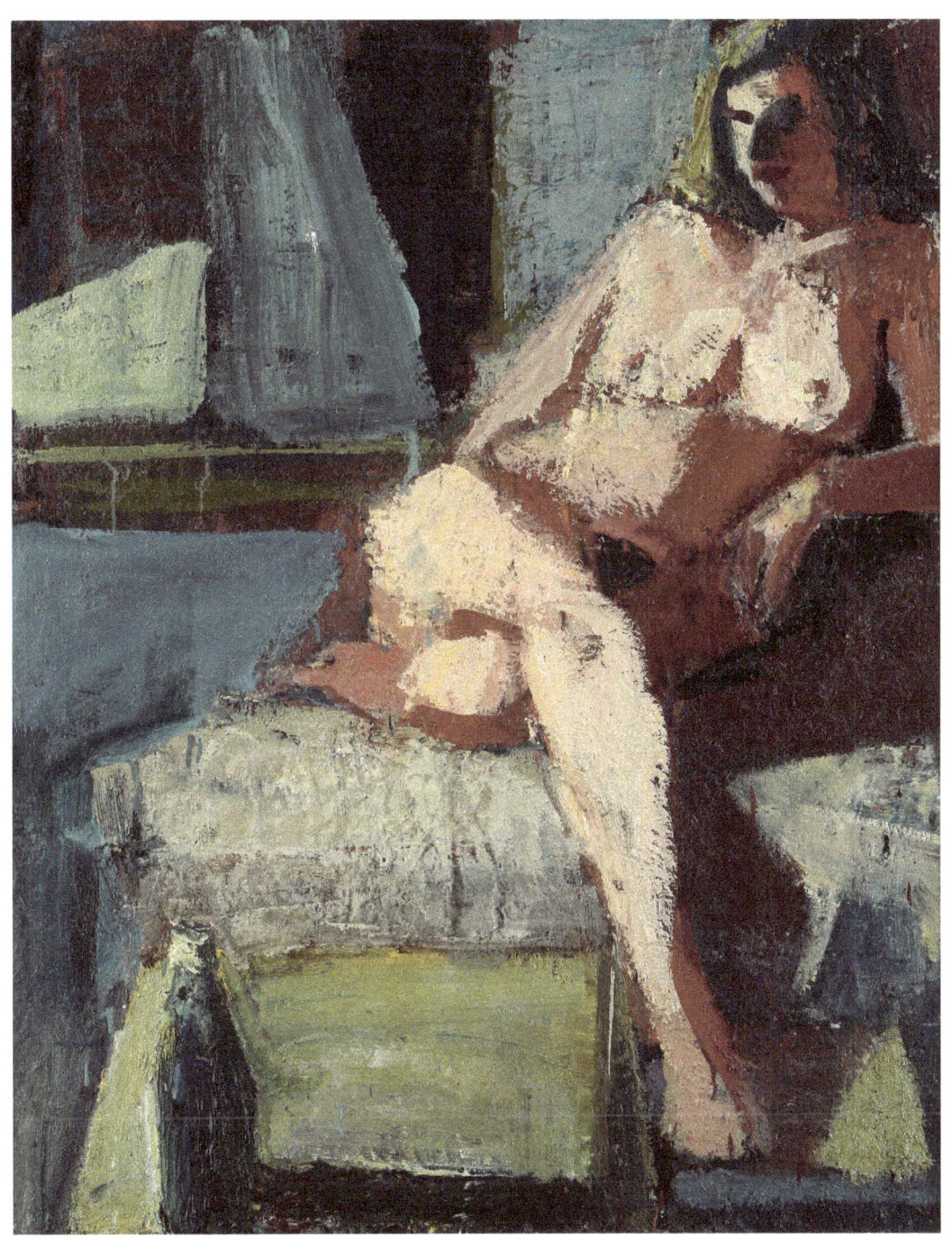

Terry St. John, *Nude, Summer*, 2005, Oil on canvas, 60 x4 8 in.

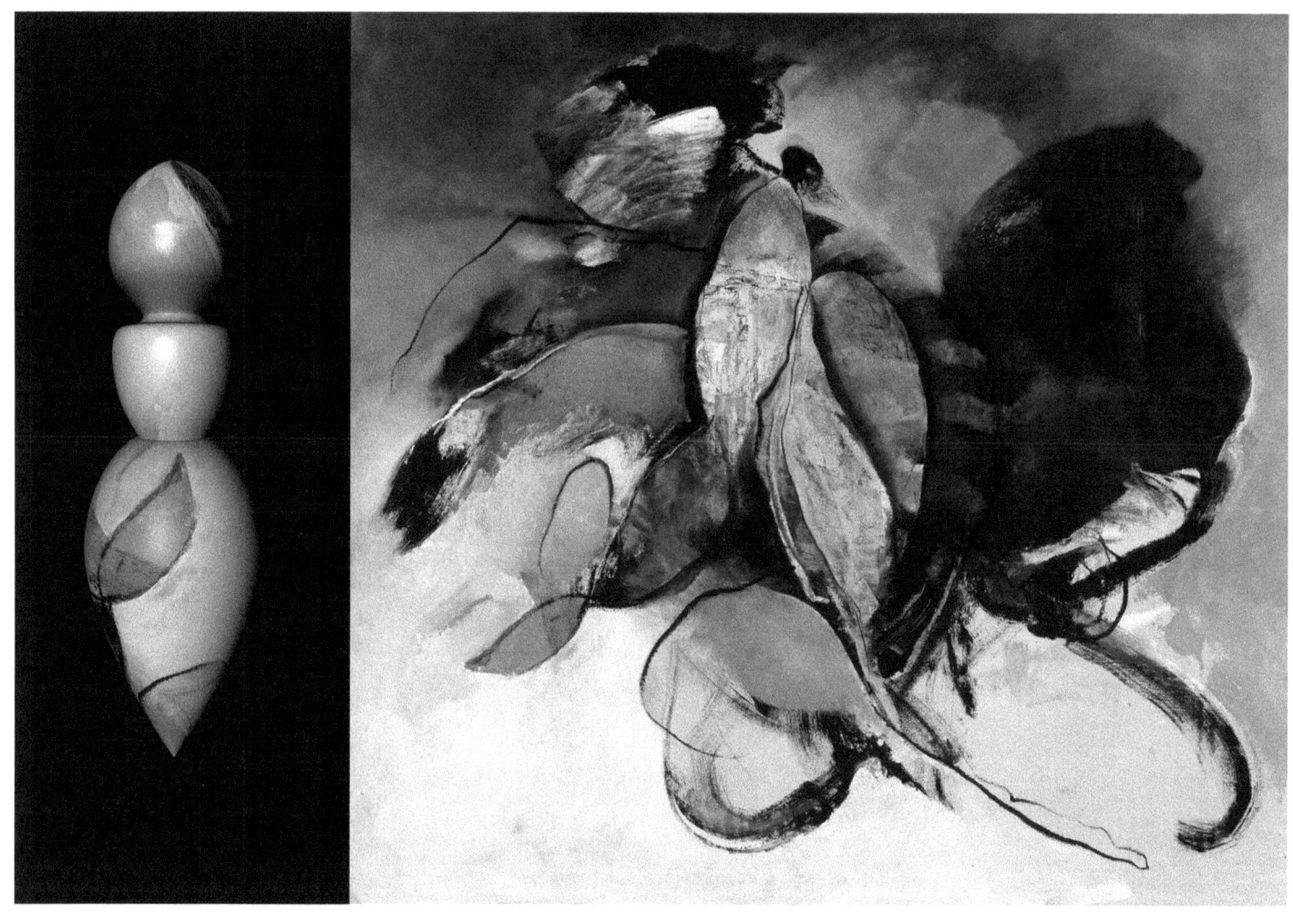

Kim Thoman, *Venus of Taos 1*, 2010, Pigment and oil, 42 x 66 in.

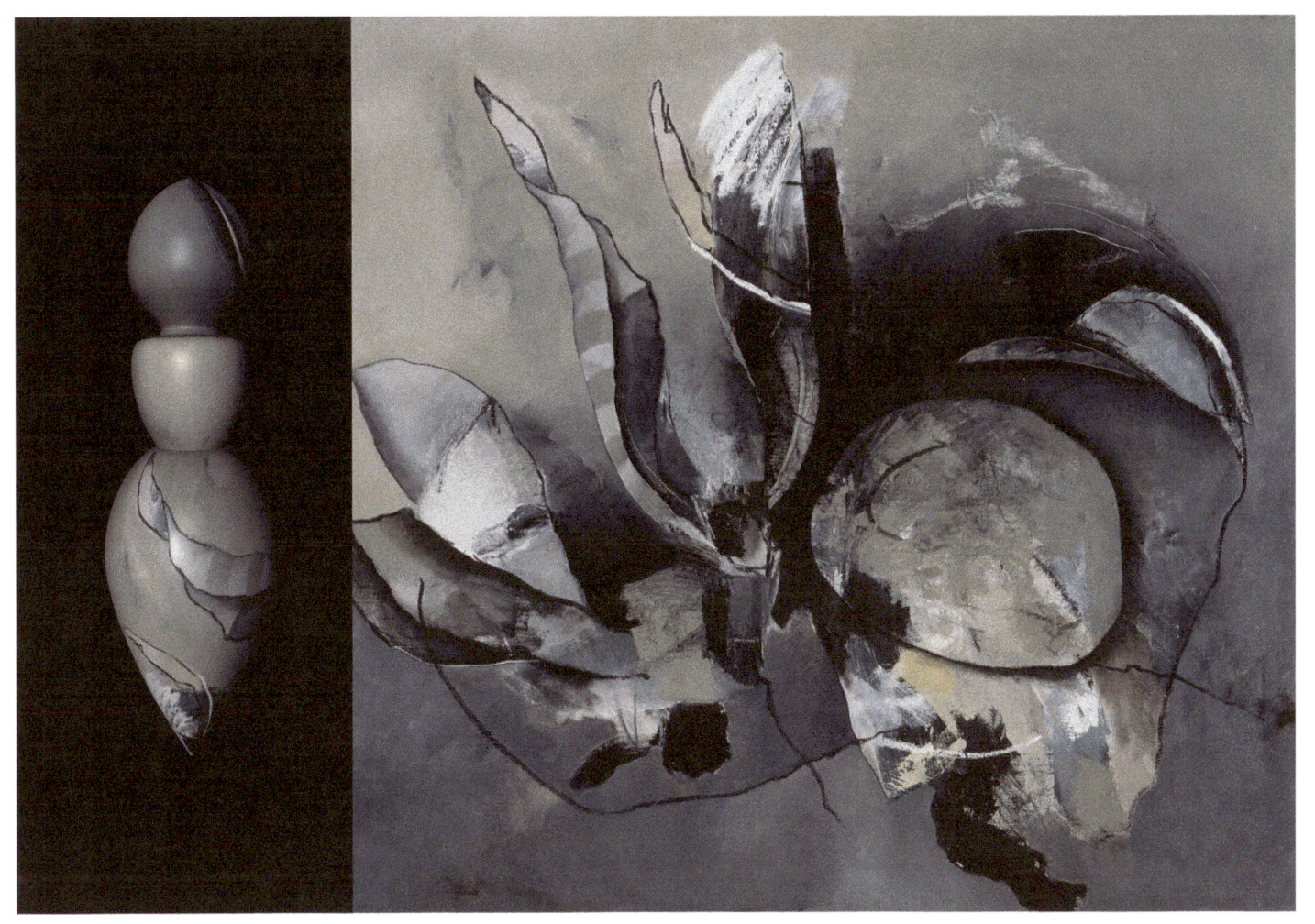

Kim Thoman, *Venus of Taos 2*, 2010, Pigment and oil, 42 x 66 in.

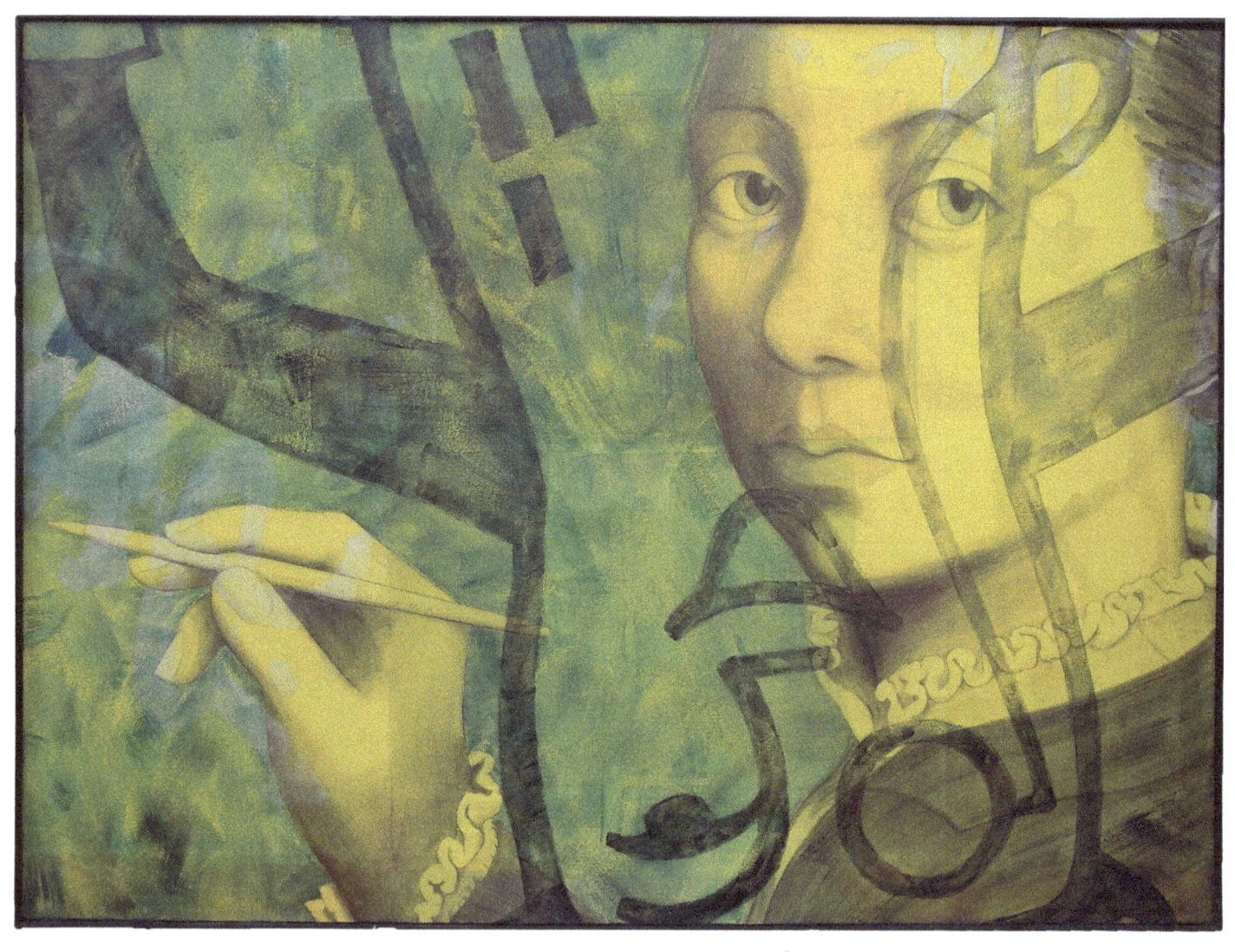

Genn Toffey, *Sofonisba Anguissola*, Oil over acrylic and pencil, 44 x 60 in.

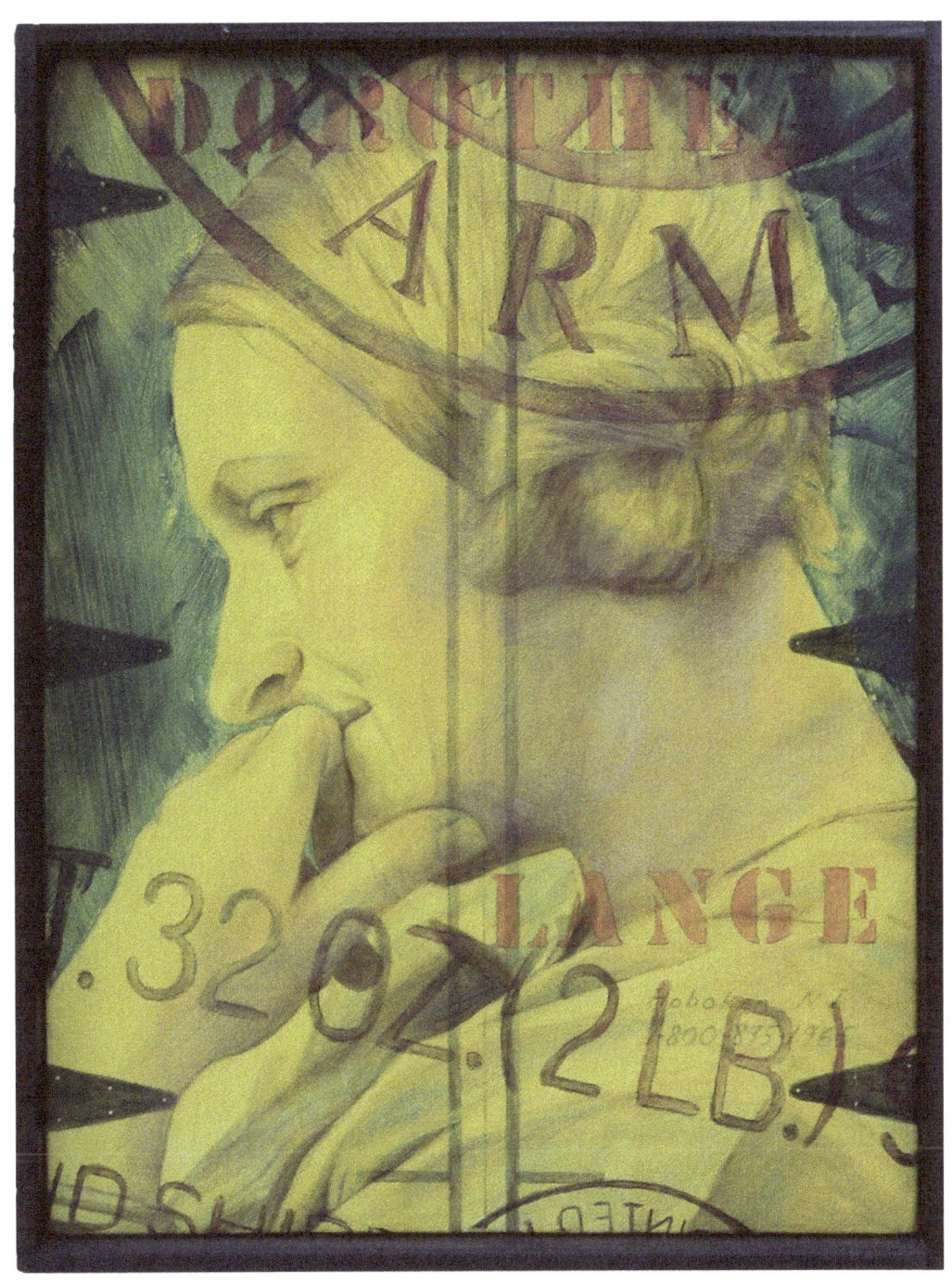

Genn Toffey, *Dorothea Lange*, Oil over acrilic and pencil, 12 x 9 in.

Sandy Walker, *Inwood l*, 2011, Woodblock print printed on paper, Edition of 10, 48 x 36 in. image on 50 x 38 in. paper pinrted at KALA

Sandy Walker, *Inwood ll*, 2011, Woodblock print printed on paper, Edition of 10, 48 x 36 in. image on 50 x 38 in. paper pinrted at KALA

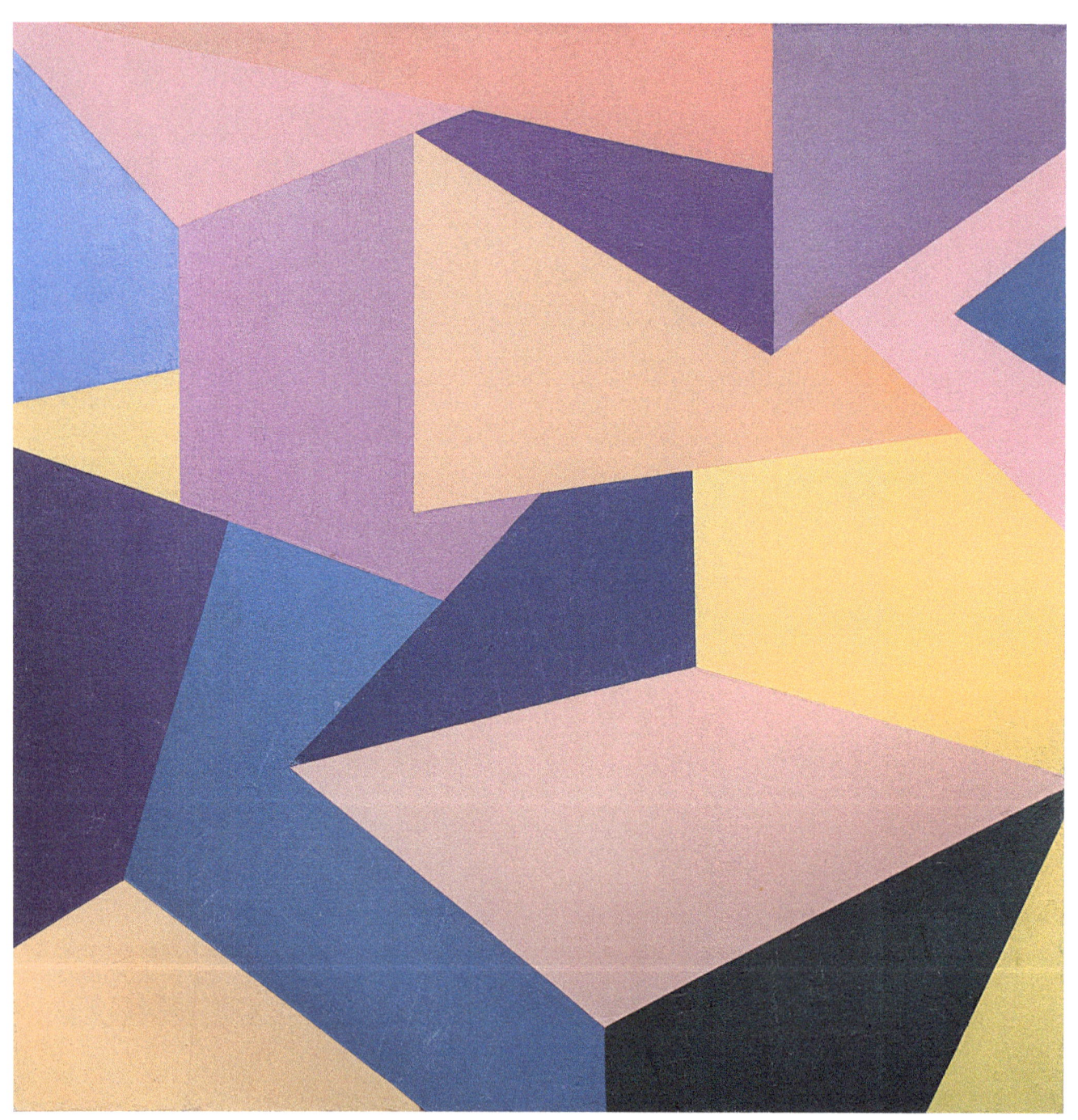

Carl Worth, *Sanctuary*, 2011-12, Acrylic on canvas, 36 x 36 in.

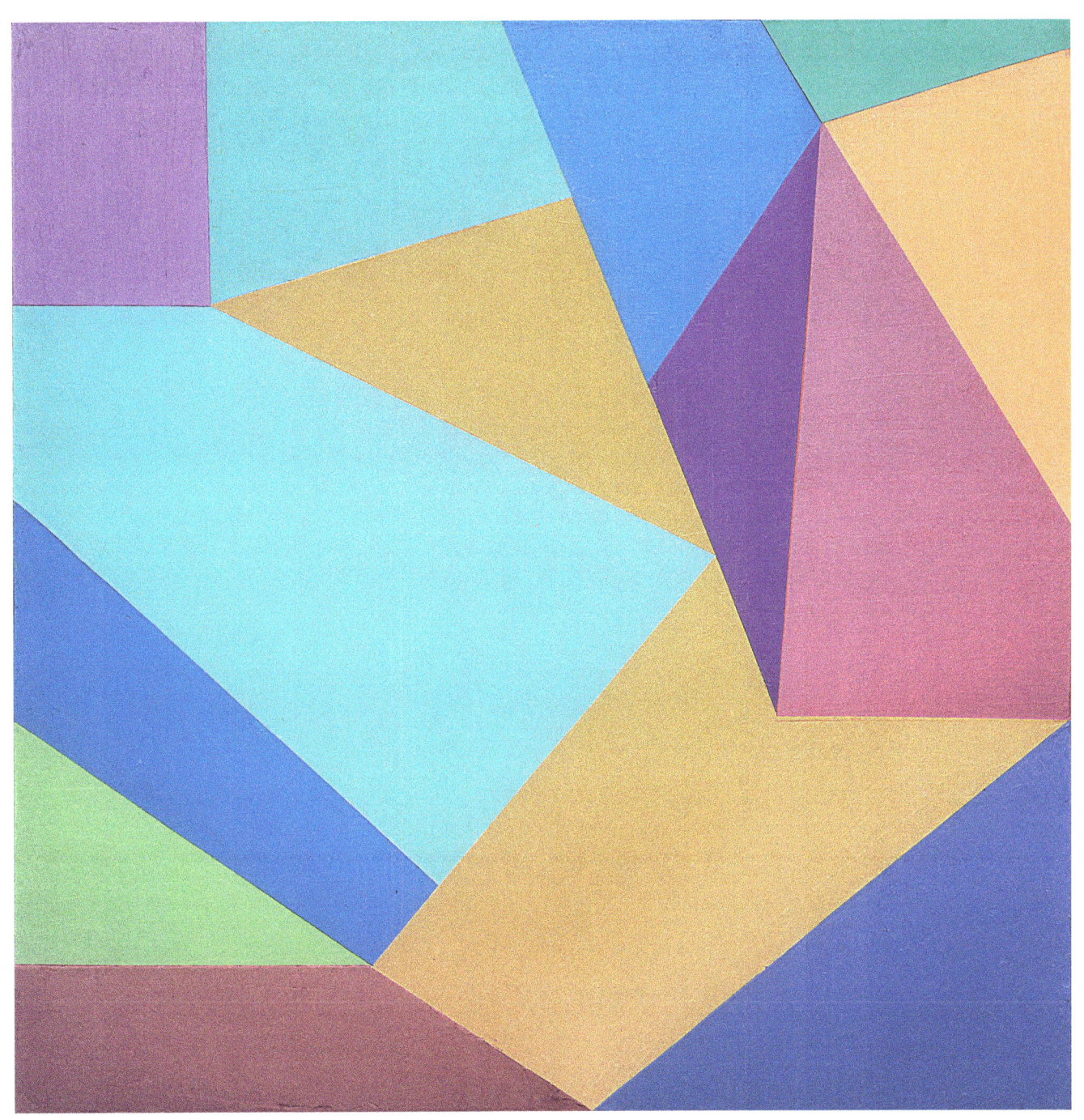

Carl Worth, *Here's Looking at Euclid*, 2009-12, 36 x 35 in.

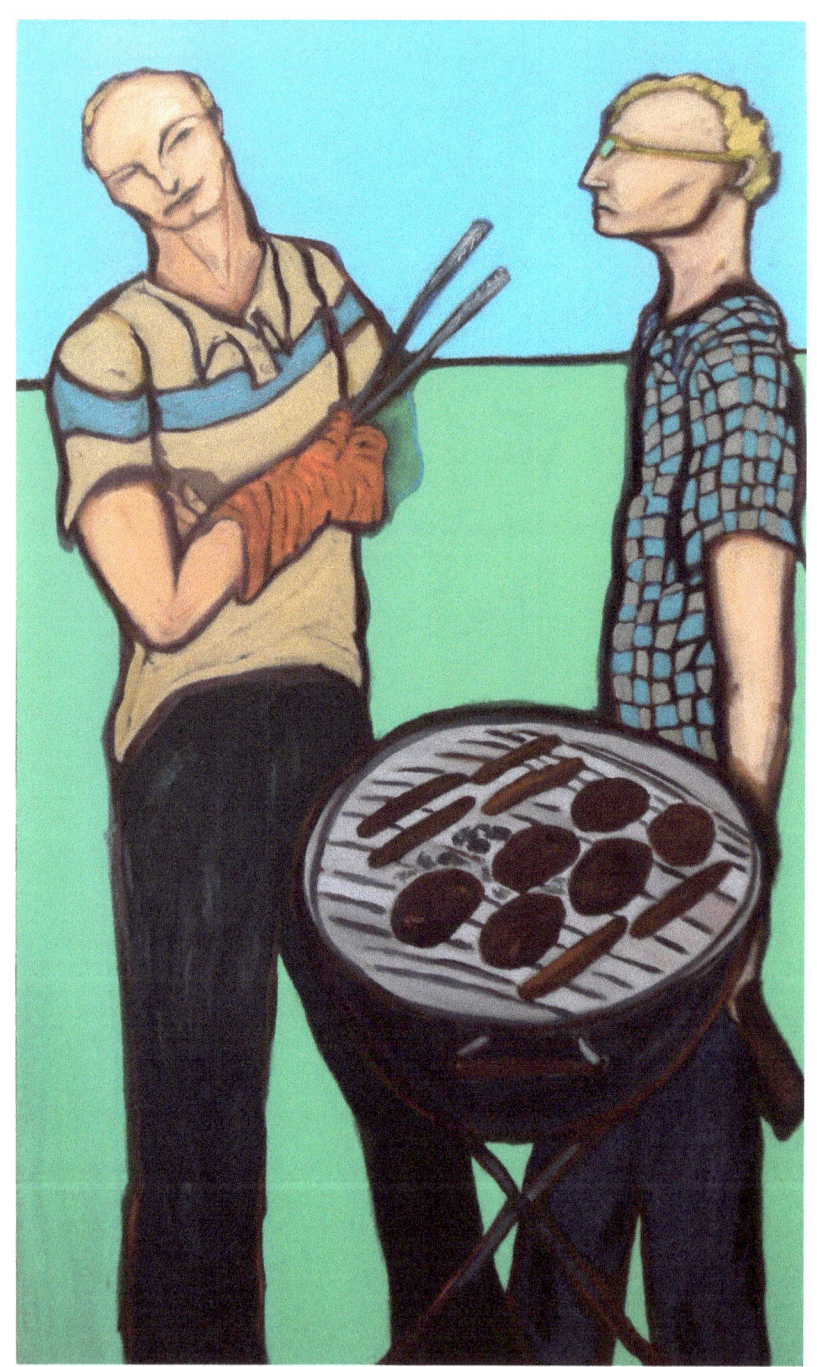

Jan Wurm, *Grilled*, 2012, Oil on canvas, 60 x 36 in.

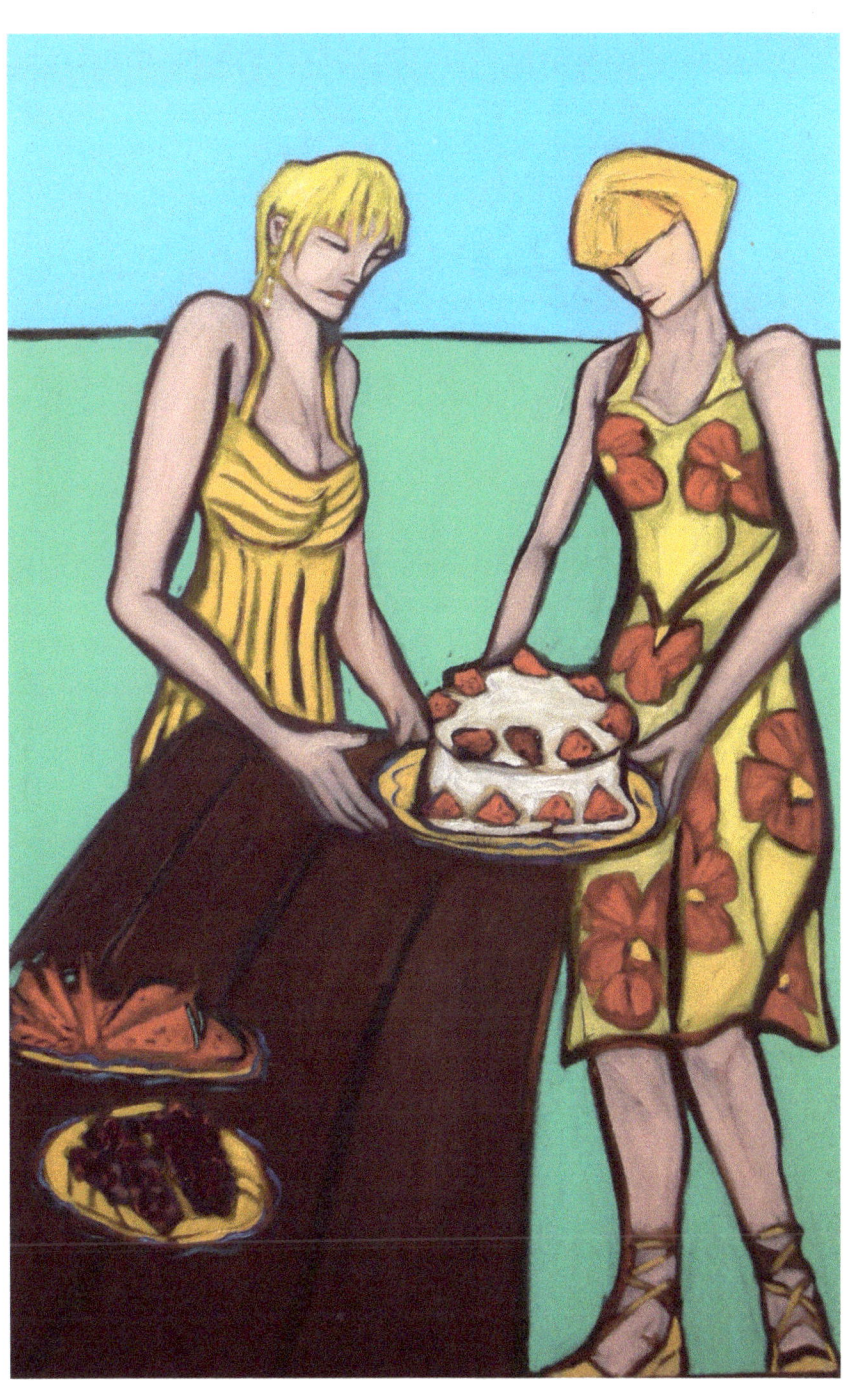

Jan Wurm, *Dessert*, 2012, Oil on canvas, 60 x 36 in.

TheBreakfast Group included

Patricia Bengston-Jones
Jeanette Bokour
Edythe Bresnahan
Jerry Carlin
K. Casida
Bruce Chaban
June Felter
Donna Fenstermaker
Lin Fischer
John Friedman
Nancy Genn
Katie Hawkinson
Barbara Hazard
Anthony Holdsworth
Stan Huncilman
Carol Ladewig
Marvin Lipofsky
P.G. Meier
Arthur Monroe
Guillermo Pulido
Loren Rehbock
Bill Rosen
Richard Sargent
Foad Satterfield
Robert Simons
Joeseph Slusky
Terry St. John
Kim Thoman
Genn Toffey
Sandy Walker
Carl Worth
Jan Wurm

www.ingramcontent.com/pod-product-compliance
Lightning Source LLC
Chambersburg PA
CBHW040544220526
45473CB00016B/3013